Cats Don't Bark

Cats Don't Bark

A GUIDE TO KNOWING WHO YOU ARE, ACCEPTING WHO YOU ARE NOT, AND LIVING YOUR UNIQUE PURPOSE

SHANE HIPPS

CENTER STREET

New York Boston Nashville

Center Street
Hachette Book Group
1290 Avenue of the Americas
New York, NY 10104

www.CenterStreet.com

Printed in the United States of America

RRD-C (Split)

First edition: October 2015

10 9 8 7 6 5 4 3 2 1

Center Street is a division of Hachette Book Group, Inc. The Center Street name and logo are trademarks of Hachette Book Group, Inc.

Library of Congress Cataloging-in-Publication Data

Hipps, Shane, 1956–
Cats don't bark : a guide to knowing who you are, accepting who you are not, and living your unique purpose / Shane Hipps. — First Edition.
pages cm
Summary: "At some point in life everyone is compelled to ask the primordial question—Why am I here? How we answer that question determines whether or not we will discover our true calling in life and harness our full professional, personal, and spiritual potential. Many counterfeit voices will offer an answer, but the one true voice whispers from the inside. CATS DON'T BARK provides powerful techniques to help the reader listen for the "One Voice" and find the courage to follow it. This is a book about discovering who we are, accepting who we are not, and cultivating the habits we need to discover and embrace who we were meant to be." — Provided by publisher.
Includes bibliographical references.
ISBN 978-1-4555-2203-3 (hardback) — ISBN 978-1-4555-2205-7 (ebook)
1. Self-actualization (Psychology) 2. Motivation (Psychology) 3. Happiness. I. Title.

BF637.S4.H57 2015
248.4—dc23

2015025605

For Bahar,
my dream come true

For Harper and Hadley,
my teachers

You carry
All the ingredients
To turn your life into a nightmare—
Don't mix them!

You have all the genius
To build a swing in your backyard
For God.

That sounds
Like a hell of a lot more fun.
Let's start laughing, drawing blueprints,
Gathering our talented friends…

You carry all the ingredients
To turn your existence into joy,

Mix them, mix
Them!

—Hafiz

CONTENTS

Cats Don't Bark

1

WHY AM I HERE?

A gorgeous thirty-foot midnight blue touring boat with a stunning profile and an unusual deck clad entirely in mahogany with maple inlays sat in the water before me. It wasn't flashy, but it was utterly arresting. There I stood, feeling out of place, on a private dock at a party thrown by a very wealthy man on his sprawling estate. I was there by chance. On the other side of the dock behind me sat an enormous three-story yacht, but for some reason I couldn't take my eyes off the smaller touring boat. Just then the host walked up to greet me. I turned casually to make conversation and hopefully appear to belong.

"I've never seen a boat like this," I said. "It's beautiful."

"Thanks. Yeah, I really love the way it sits in the water. Nothing quite like it."

He mentioned a few other unique attributes that were lost on me, but he didn't seem interested in bragging. Then he politely thanked me for coming and continued making his rounds with the other guests.

Later I was talking to one of the guests at the party and I asked if he had seen that particular boat.

"Amazing, isn't it?" he replied. "Do you know how much that thing costs?"

I guessed around $150,000 (an inflated estimate, I reasoned).

"Not even close. That's a *Riva*!" He laughed.

This meant nothing to me.

He could see that. "It's an Italian-made boat. There are only three of these in the country and only about a hundred made each year. A Riva like this would cost at least a million dollars."

My jaw dropped. It was certainly a work of art, and clearly well crafted, but I would have never guessed it. This was a simple lesson in economics. In this case, much of the value was determined by a limited supply. The price was derived not just from craftsmanship and materials, but from the boat's rarity. I felt somehow special to be in the presence of something so valuable and so rare.

Then again, it was just a boat, even if it was one in a hundred. By contrast, an estimated seven billion people are living on the earth today. That's a lot of people. Of all those billions of people, not one—not a single one—is like you. That means you are one in seven billion—a true one of a kind. In other words, a Riva has nothing on you. It's an impressive stat. But let's go back in time for a moment and consider all of human history. From this perspective the number looks a little different. By some estimates nearly 160 billion people have lived on this earth since the beginning of human history. In all that time, in all those people, no one has ever been like you. And in all the billions of people who have yet to be born, not a single one will ever be like you. No one sees the world the way you do, tastes food the way you do, laughs like you, speaks like you, is shaped like you, appreciates music like you, plays like you, creates like you, or wants exactly what you want in life.

You are completely, utterly, and incalculably unique. And here you are—walking, talking, thinking, feeling, and doing. Right now you are. I am. And one day we won't be, not like this. While you walk the earth, you are worth more than all the wealth in the world. You are a genuine miracle, and yet most of the time we are oblivious to this fact. But every once in a while something peeks into our mundane activities and we recognize it. We have a keen awareness that this life is an extraordinary moment. We know somehow—even when life is difficult—we've been given a precious gift. It is the reason that everyone at some point is compelled to ask that primordial question—*Why am I here?*

Beneath our conscious awareness, we can feel there must be something more to our being here.

There must be a reason for the extravagant gift of existence. It can't all be just a cosmic accident. And so we search for the purpose that pulses beneath the surface.

The question can be posed in terms that are detached and philosophical or studied and existential. But my interest is only in the personal nature of the question: *Why am I, [INSERT YOUR NAME], here right now? What am I supposed to be doing with this life?* These are the most important questions we can ask in our lifetime.

You will find no shortage of answers to these questions. Scores of books have been written on the subject. If you are a religious person, your religious leaders and sacred texts will gladly offer a set of answers to you. Then we have our parents, spouses, partners, friends, children, teachers, advertisers, employers, and cultures, all of whom will eagerly give direction and advice. Most of the answers offered by others remove ambiguity from the search. They answer the questions for us. At first, this may seem to be a great relief, but sooner or later most of us come to realize a very important truth: in reality, no one can answer these questions for you. The reason is that the answers do not come in words from the outside, but rather as an experience, an intuition, a gut sense from within.

THE QUEST

The word *question* is an interesting one. It shares the same root as the word *quest*. Both come from a Latin word that means "to seek." The fundamental *questions* (*Why am I here right now? What am I supposed to do with this life?*) drive our most basic *quest* in life. Your quest is yours and yours alone. This book does not answer the questions for you, but it will help you find answers. It offers new ways of seeing, fresh tools, and proven practices designed to serve as companions as you embark on your quest. Think of this book as a compass and map in the wilderness. I do not pretend to know your starting point or your destination. But I have found some very powerful aids no matter where you are or where you're going. They work.

Think of this book as a compass and map in the wilderness.

I come by these tools honestly. I've had an unconventional career path with several unexpected turns. I started as a strategic planner in advertising, where I worked on brands ranging from Porsche to Harrah's to Formica. Then I did what every ad guy does: I went to seminary. After that I did the one thing I never thought I would do—become the pastor of a small

Mennonite church. And later I served as the pastor of a megachurch. Today I'm involved in corporate leadership development, executive coaching, speaking, and writing.

That's just my professional life. My personal life is no less linear. Each one of my transitions and decisions could be made into a book all its own. Some of these reinventions were easier than others. Each one came with a cost, as well as a gift. Through them all I have been a devoted student of the process of finding and living my purpose. At times I have been both inspired by clarity and utterly lost. I have been a coward and deceived myself along the way. I have also learned to listen carefully and live courageously and creatively.

None of this is a judgment, nor is it self-congratulating. I'm simply stating what is. All of it fits in the story just as it should. Some may read the story of your life (or mine) through a lens of judgment. This is understandable—we've been taught rights and wrongs, goods and bads, morals and values. These are useful for many aspects of life. However, judgment and self-condemnation have no place in the process of purpose. They are the fastest way to undermine the first and most important ingredient in uncovering your purpose.

Judgment and self-condemnation have no place in the process of purpose.

HONESTY REQUIRED

The cornerstone of this entire process is honesty. We must be willing to be honest first with ourselves. Nothing undermines our honesty like judgment or condemnation, which fuel guilt and shame. When we deem something in us as bad or unworthy, we quickly learn to hide it from ourselves and others. We set up defenses for fear of exclusion, embarrassment, or rejection. This is when self-deception sets in. It causes all of our desires to submerge into the clandestine land of the unconscious. There they remain buried, obscuring our true desires, our motives, and our purpose. Our unconscious patterns serve as a puppet master dictating and distorting our movements. In the process we cheat ourselves, steal away our true inner joy, and live a life that is not our own.

Throughout my experiences, I made myself a student of techniques that could help me align with my purpose and listen for direction that comes from within. I also learned a lot about the cost when you ignore such direction, and the reward when you follow it. This process isn't just about career or life choices; those are only the surface changes. Beneath these shifts are basic alterations in our being, the uncovering and expansion of our true

Finding direction and living with purpose are as much about discovering who we are as they are about accepting what we're not.

nature, the truth about who we are. Finding direction and living with purpose are as much about discovering who we are as they are about accepting what we're not.

Which brings me to the title of the book—*Cats Don't Bark*. This is the simplest way I could distill the common misunderstanding people encounter in everything from relationship problems to finding and living a purpose. In short, most of us spend some part of our lives pretending to be something we are not, and expecting others to do the same.

This is understandable. Our lives begin as an imitative process. We learn whom to be and how to behave by mirroring our parents. We learn gender roles by mimicking Mom or Dad. We see that when we act like Mom or Dad, we get positive feedback. Later we learn to imitate other people we want to like us. Our peers, possible partners, and bosses all present us with opportunities to ignore or deny our true nature and adopt or react to the vision they have. Alternatively, we may seek to exert control and manipulate others so that they are more like us, insisting they become something they are not in order to make us feel better.

Eventually, though, we learn a simple truth: We don't like living according to what others want or expect from us. And it's tiring to force, cajole, or manipulate others into speaking or behaving in ways we prefer.

The path of discovering and living our purpose is a process of coming to terms with who we really are—and what we truly want—and accepting that fact as self-evident without judgment. It's also a process of accepting others for who they are and not trying to entice or force them to be something they are not. When we do this, we soon come to the truth in a drama-free way, as simply as observing that cats don't bark. (Why would they? It's not their nature.) And the sooner we accept this fact about ourselves and others, the sooner the drama can stop and the faster we will be on a path to living our purpose and creating the life we want most.

TO CREATE CONSCIOUSLY

As a pastor, I spent most of my time trying to untangle the mess religion has made of the word *God.* I found that word always seemed to come with a 747 full of baggage. However, I live with a deep awareness that I am utterly dependent upon something much more vast and powerful than

> *I live with a deep awareness that I am utterly dependent upon something much more vast and powerful than I am.*

I am. I depend on it for my very existence and everything in it. It is the source of everything I have and everything I am. It is the very breath that dances in me. Without it, I am in a box in the ground.

I acknowledge that most people use the word *God* to label that reality. So if you want to use the word *God*, that's fine with me. But it goes by many names: Life, the Source, All That Is, Infinite Intelligence, Inspiration, the Muse, the Holy Spirit, Christ, the Universe, Consciousness, Existence, Breath, Divinity, Love, the Uncreated Creator—the list goes on. Some of these names will resonate for you; others will sound too religious, New Agey, or vague. That's OK because this power doesn't need a name. Feel free to choose a name that works best for you, or no name at all.

The name is not nearly as important as the direct experience of this power. At some moment in life you have experienced inspiration, an intuitive hunch, deep appreciation, joy, a feeling of being in the "zone," or unexpected creativity that seemed to come from somewhere outside you. It was bigger than you, and when it came through you, it felt exhilarating. Each and every one of these moments is an experience of the Source of Life. You and I came into this world with unlimited access to an extraordinary creative power.

In the simplest terms, we were made to make.

The object of our creation is not at issue here. It could be a painting, a rocket, a relationship, a family, a business, a spreadsheet, an empire, a policy, a curriculum, a cure, or a meal. Whatever it is, we are in a state of constant creation whether we know it or not. The question is, are we creating the life we want *consciously*? Are we awake to the things we are creating? In a very real sense our purpose is not just something we are here to find; it is also something we get to create. With this in mind, the question *Why am I here?* takes on a slightly different tone. Another way to ask the question might be, "How do I want to create my life?" We are here to create something that has never existed before. So what do you want to create?

> *In a very real sense our purpose is not just something we are here to find; it is also something we get to create.*

AN INNER "YES"

I sat across from my boss at his desk. He was a tall, barrel-chested man with a full jaw and thin blond hair. "Why are you committing career suicide?" he asked. I had just informed him that I would be leaving advertising to attend seminary—not exactly a standard next step in career advancement.

I understood his confusion. In my head I built an answer designed to steel my resolve. But it smacked of high-minded moralizing and condescension. It went something like this:

"Advertising is a form of coercion that makes use of the most sophisticated kinds of deception wrapped in seduction. It is the engine that drives the worst parts of consumer culture. It creates values at odds with..." And so on.

Looking back, I don't entirely dismiss the rant. Except that it had little to do with my actual reason for leaving a fun job that paid well. In reality, leaving advertising was not some act of nobility, but it's what I told myself and others and how I presented myself. I wanted to be someone other than who I was. There's something empowering, albeit misguided, about playing the role of a high holy hero driven by moral conviction. This stance made it a little easier to leave something I enjoyed.

In reality, a subtle dis-ease had begun to emerge in me over the course of a year. Something I couldn't explain was nudging me. It didn't make sense at first. Sometimes I wrote it off as just being overworked and feeling underpaid. Other days I thought of it as the cost of doing business or dealing with irritating clients and coworkers. But one thing was sure—I wasn't where I wanted to be. I remember asking a question: If I died today, would I have lived doing what I was made to do? The answer was a resounding no.

If I died today, would I have lived doing what I was made to do?

It was more like I had developed some strange allergy to a food I liked. Though I enjoyed the taste, I felt compelled to spit it out. A voice inside was saying, "You weren't made for this. It's time for something else." Unfortunately it didn't tell me what that was. Back then, I felt a strange affinity for studying theology, culture, technology, and psychology in my leisure time. So seminary became an unexpected but natural next step as I began the process of finding my purpose. But at the time, following my curiosity without knowing where it was leading, and not following a strategic life plan, felt like a risky decision.

The question my boss wanted to know was, why? Frankly, I wanted an answer to the same question. All I knew was that for some time something deep inside me insisted advertising wasn't what I was supposed to be doing. Deep down I knew whatever ladder I was climbing was leaning against the wrong wall. I was not doing what I was made to do. In that moment I knew I had to plan my departure and forge a different path. While that was the feeling, in reality I also knew my being in advertising wasn't a mistake. I hadn't taken a wrong turn and gotten lost. It was all part of the mysterious path of purpose, contributing experiences and skills that both clarified and expanded who I was.

This is one of my earliest adult memories of connecting with a strong sense of direction in life. It became the first of many twists and turns, all of which have led me back to myself. Until then, everything had been planned for me, as is the case for many middle- and upper-class people in the Western world. Other than deciding which college to attend or which major to choose, many of us face few significant decisions during our school years. Every major crossroad is mapped out before you get to it, until you graduate. Then the crossroads only become clear after you've passed through them, with no warning that they are coming and no accompanying ritual or ceremony.

The decision to attend seminary meant a cross-country move from the frozen tundra of Minnesota to sunny Southern California. That little detail made the adventure all the more exciting. Soon after arriving and getting settled, I eased my way into the unknown. The path remained unclear for several years. I thoroughly enjoyed seminary and the studies, but none of it seemed to lead me any closer to my next step in life. In time I found myself in an unexpected depression. The question my boss had asked me started to make more sense. Why did I commit career suicide for seminary? If I didn't want to be a pastor, then why was I in seminary?

I found myself adrift in a sea of ambivalence. I had no idea what I was supposed to do. The natural roles for seminary graduates—pastor, chaplain, professor, missionary—didn't appeal to me. So I went looking for help. I talked with mentors, a therapist, chaplains, and several of my professors. None of them had the answers to my fundamental questions: *What am I supposed to do? Why am I here?* It's not that they didn't try to help, but they couldn't possibly have known the answers.

Eventually I found a guide who pointed me in a new direction. She showed me unusual techniques that led me to an unexpected place. In time I learned that the answers to the questions I was asking come only from within.

In time I learned that the answers to the questions I was asking come only from within.

The answer ultimately comes as an experience. That feeling you get when things line up and suddenly you feel at home. When I first learned how to tune a guitar, it took a while to figure out how a given string was supposed to sound. I would bend the notes up and down, straining to find the right frequency, usually passing through the right range and then losing it again. Eventually, with enough practice, I could hear when the string found its home. The same feeling exists in each of us. The innate birthright of joy—an inner frequency that sings, "Yes!"

That experience is why we are here. We are here in part to feel the pleasure of the One who created us and join in the act of creation. There is nothing more blissful on the planet than the experience of being in tune with the Source of Life within us. That feeling of inspired action and creation is the infallible indicator for whether we are living our purpose. This will also present many lessons along the way, chances to grow and expand our being. Our invitation and opportunity is to allow Love to live through us—unobstructed, unbound, fearless, and free. Anytime we find ourselves asking why we are here, it means we have simply forgotten our birthright of joy, of peace, of limitless fulfillment. And the question will continue to return each time we forget. It will return as a reminder that more joy, bliss, and possibilities are always available to us.

2

WHY IS THE ANSWER SO HARD TO FIND?

Most of us have to spend time learning, and in some cases *unlearning*, the answer to the question *Why am I here?* Some portion of life is spent in a state of unknowing, wondering, wandering, and questioning. In one sense, this is a deliberate feature of our existence. If I offered you a glass of water when you weren't thirsty, you would have no interest in it. But if I encountered you after a long walk in the desert, the glass of water would be like gold. You would be keenly aware of a need where one did not exist before. When we are thirsty and we drink water, appreciation is the natural response. The experience of not knowing is partly there to activate a thirst in us. That sense that there has to be something more, something we are missing and vaguely longing for, must be present to fuel the quest. Finding, creating, and living our purpose requires energy, focus, and attention. The drive for more is the built-in mechanism to accelerate the quest.

This is not only a process of discovery, but also a process of creation. We do not begin by unveiling a fully formed purpose. We listen for direction, or desire, and create more on our way. Calling is

Calling is sometimes thought of only in terms of destiny or predestination. However, I prefer to set calling in the context of extraordinary freedom.

sometimes thought of only in terms of destiny or predestination. However, I prefer to set calling in the context of extraordinary freedom. Creative free choice is built into the process. This process of creation is as important as the outcome. It is actually part of the joy, the gift of Love. Love would never want to rob us of that experience. If a painter could snap her fingers and a work of art on canvas would appear instantaneously, how much would she enjoy that process? Perhaps the first few times it would be exciting. But part of the joy is in the discovery, exploration, inspiration, and learning that come with the creative process itself.

Because we are not only finding but also creating our purpose in life, our purpose is never complete. On one level our purpose is always in the making—moving, unfolding, ending, being reborn, and expanding. Our task is to develop the skill to listen for it, respond to it, and live it moment by moment.

When it comes to the hiddenness of purpose, there is one other ingredient. Not long ago my daughters, Harper and Hadley, who were eight and five respectively, came rushing into my room, breathless and grinning.

"Dad, come here! You have to come here and see this!" Harper blurted out.

I stood up to follow them, when Hadley grabbed my hand and said, "You have to close your eyes." Under normal conditions this would have been an easy request, but it was not so simple as it meant a walk across the house and upstairs to her room.

"Keep your eyes closed. Are they closed?"

"Yes."

To avoid major injury, I peeked a few times. She was far more interested in getting us to the destination quickly than she was in helping me safely navigate obstacles on the way. I had to look after myself.

"Don't open them until I tell you," she said.

"I won't," I said, lying.

As we approached her room, with safety assured, I kept my eyes closed. In a singsong voice she said, "Wait...wait...wait...." Then she carefully positioned me in just the right spot.

Both girls shouted, "OK. Open them!"

I opened my eyes to see they had created a fort in their room by using sofa cushions, blankets, and a bed. The fort was populated with stuffed animals and other assorted toys that were neatly organized. They squealed with delight when they saw the look of surprise on my face. This little game happens often when they make things, especially if it's something they make as a gift for me. They love to surprise me, and I love to be surprised. For them the surprise is part of the present.

I feel the same way at Christmas with them. I love to deliver an unexpected gift to see what their reaction will be. It would never occur to me to open a present for them or tell them weeks before Christmas what they are getting. That surprise belongs to them; it's part of the gift.

Life is the same way. The Universe delights in our experience of surprise and the unexpected gift we get to unwrap. For this reason, we must learn to allow the experience of not knowing to serve as a prelude to the joy of surprise. From this posture, the experience of the unknown deepens anticipation. Times of transition become pregnant with possibility and expectation.

The Universe delights in our experience of surprise and the unexpected gift we get to unwrap.

WHITE NOISE AND THE ONE VOICE

The hidden part of purpose is set up like a bit of a treasure hunt. It is designed that way for our enjoyment. However, the quest for our purpose can also be elusive and opaque for different reasons. This happens when we get in our own way. We have developed habits of ignoring and discounting the subtlety of inner guidance, which is always available.

In the north, winters are long. Days are spent mostly indoors, and the air takes on an artificial quality. Like most things in life you get used to it—sort of. But not long after Christmas, the monochromatic gray hues of winter start to weigh heavy. My mind fidgets and my bones get antsy. I want those green shoots to crack the ice and reveal life again. Eventually it happens; it always does. The final thaw breaks winter's back in two. Sometime in late spring there is a day when it feels like summer.

On that day, I drive with the radio up and the windows down. It is pure liberation. The wind rushes in and fresh air fills the car and my lungs. All is well in the world. Everything is perfect until I get on the highway. When the wind picks up, a competition ensues. Soon, the white noise of the wind drowns out the music on the radio. The music is still playing, but the noise of the wind masks the notes. Eventually I have to decide whether I want to hear the music or feel the wind. At first the wind wins. But as warm days wear on, my desire shifts. I miss the music. As soon as I roll up the windows and shut out the white noise of the wind and the world outside, the song inside comes through with clarity.

In the same way, we must learn to understand the difference between white noise and what I call the One Voice. Pursuing and creating our purpose is about decisions both small and large. It doesn't matter what we hope to create. It could be an education, a work of art, a relationship, a family, a living space, a career, or better health. In all of these creations, we make decisions. With each one, advice comes from the four corners of the earth. The agendas of others are not difficult to find. Sometimes these voices are unanimous. Other times they are dissonant. When the voices are at odds, they jockey for primacy. The great challenge is in knowing what to make of all the information.

We must learn to understand the difference between white noise and what I call the One Voice.

Some voices seeking to influence our choices come from the outside. Parents, friends, spouses, children, advertisers, books, authority figures, and others all have opinions and grand plans for our lives. All of them want us to want, do, or be something. Some will convince us that our well-being depends upon us wanting what they want us to want. They apply considerable pressure even if unconsciously.

Other voices come from inside. Our ambitions, addictions, ego delusions, patterns, personality preferences, wishes, biological impulses, and messages we have internalized from childhood all rattle around in the echo chamber of the mind. As each one arises, it steals our attention. All these voices carry a certain weight. To varying degrees they guide us like the bit in a horse's mouth, some even coming to serve as blinders. All of this, both inside and out, is the white noise of life. If we heed it too much, we may end up walking a path chosen by others and fail to find our own. In short, we would live a lie.

Among these voices, one is different. It is subtle and rarely overbearing, yet it is uncompromising and persistent. It is as humble and powerful as a drop of water. It is easily overlooked. But give it time and it can carve vast canyons out of mountains. Many voices will masquerade as this voice. The One Voice does not usually start in audible form, but instead as a deep longing or desire, an intuitive awareness, a synchronicity, or a subtle hunch in your gut. It comes from the deepest recesses of our being, not the frantic and tumultuous surface waters of the mind. No fear is found in this tenor. It is courageous, trusting, and full of love.

The One Voice does not usually start in audible form, but instead as a deep longing or desire, an intuitive awareness, a synchronicity, or a subtle hunch in your gut.

At some point in life, everyone becomes aware of a nascent longing, something deep inside that nudges us. It may confirm we are on track with a feeling of exhilaration, or it may tell us we aren't doing what we're made to do or that we're off course with a sense of dread or discomfort. It tells us a particular path is coming to an end and a new one must begin. That is the One Voice. In one sense this Voice is more often experienced as a feeling. In fact, it is the language of our inner being, which means our feelings are an excellent indicator of how aligned we are with the One Voice.

> *Our feelings are an excellent indicator of how aligned we are with the One Voice.*

This Voice calls out from the center of us. Once we identify it, we notice it speaks with quiet authority over all the others. When we hear and trust it, we know which way to go. The more we trust it and have the courage to act on its directives, the louder it becomes. The more we ignore it and refuse to follow it, the more it retreats into the white noise of life.

Listening for and living according to this Voice is the way we follow our purpose in life; it is also the source of our greatest potential, which brings us back to my little conundrum of driving with the windows down. Ultimately, any voice, other than the One Voice, merely contributes to the white noise, the cacophony of sound that drowns out the music inside. These counterfeit voices from both outside and inside put on an incredible show. They will convince us with carrots, sticks, and all manner of tricks that they are speaking on behalf of the One Voice.

When it comes to this Voice, you are the only one who can hear it. No one else can. Certain people can help you listen for it. Some can help clear away competing voices; they can even help you confirm it. But you are the only one who will actually hear the Voice. The One Voice is yours and yours alone, not your parents', not your spouse's, not your counselor's, not your teacher's, not your boss's, not your religious leader's, not your friend's, not your community's. Yours.

Twenty-first-century life is flooded with a myriad of distractions. Our "smart" phones, social media, screens, entertainment options, and work and family demands can all become sources of noise. In different ways and at different times these must be blocked out. This takes discipline and focus. The pursuit of more information, connection, and entertainment must stop long enough to let something else emerge. At first the silence may produce anxiety, even boredom. But if we are patient, just beyond

> *Unless we create the necessary breathing room from everything on the outside, the One Voice remains only a distant and inarticulate whisper.*

these the One Voice sings its song. Unless we create the necessary breathing room from everything on the outside, the One Voice remains only a distant and inarticulate whisper. Shut out the white noise, give it time, and something remarkable happens. The One Voice comes through with clarity, and direction in our life emerges. More than just doing what you're supposed to do in life, you come home and learn to know yourself, the only person you will spend the rest of your life with, the one person from whom there is no escape. Given this fact, we would be wise to get to know and make peace with that person. The rewards are startling.

The chatter of our own minds is nearly impossible to eliminate completely. So we must learn to listen through it or beyond it to gain distance. Distinguishing between two or more competing voices is a skill, like a musician tuning a string by ear. Patience and wisdom are needed to know which voice is the One Voice and which are merely contributing to white noise. Anyone can learn this skill through practice. Over time, given the right methods and motivation, we can learn to tune in to the One Voice with greater ease.

The white noise of the mind usually comes from our ego. That's the part of us designed to help us survive and provide for the basic needs of physical existence. It is highly protective and alert to threats at all times. In this regard it's a very helpful assistant through life. The ego tends to get a bad rap, but it is an essential support to our survival. The problem with the ego is when it operates beyond the realm of physical life. When it comes to matters of guidance, connecting in relationships, or living our potential, mostly it gets in the way. The ego wasn't designed for these things any more than a rolling pin was designed to cut vegetables. That doesn't make a rolling pin bad; it's just suited to a very specific task. Once we know the purpose it serves, it's helpful. Use it for anything else and we won't like the results.

The ego and the One Voice are designed for different purposes, and they sound very different. They are two different strings on a guitar; the ego has a different frequency than the One Voice. Learning to distinguish between these two vibrational frequencies is essential.

The ego and the One Voice are designed for different purposes, and they sound very different.

Your ego wants to help and will try to find its way into every part of life. It is very clever and will convincingly masquerade as the voice of guidance. But you will know it is your ego because when it comes to the important matters, it usually:

- Introduces fear or anger into decisions.
- Presents long, complex explanations or elaborate plans and scenarios.
- Becomes reactive, defensive, critical, and judgmental of you or others.
- Feeds your insecurity or, just as often, flatters you.
- Uses things that are true, but in the wrong context.
- Uses all-or-nothing thinking—everything is right or wrong or "good" or "bad."
- Leaves you feeling stressed, depleted, or down.
- Intensifies the importance of what other people think.
- Plots ways to change or manipulate the thoughts, feelings, or actions of others.

The One Voice, on the other hand:

- Tells the truth without flattery or judgment.
- Brings a sense of peace, inspiration, or comfort, even when the information is hard to hear.

- Shows concern for others without being governed by them.
- Leaves you feeling accepted, appreciated, and worthy, even when revealing your dark side.
- Is simple and concise in its message, often providing images and metaphors.
- Gives just enough light for the next step (like a lantern) rather than a ten-year plan (like a floodlight).
- Gives you complete freedom to choose your own way.
- Is always there to guide you, no matter how long you have ignored it.
- Assists or restores your integrity.

These are just some initial contours of each voice. The more familiar you become with them, the more you will find your own distinctions. The focus here is around feeling or sensing the differences, rather than thinking or reasoning them. The One Voice is not as mysterious as it sounds. In fact, it is as simple as paying attention to how you feel.

YOUR GUIDANCE SYSTEM

The two lists above involve feeling states. Our emotional life gives us important clues in life. The more we pay attention to how we feel, the more

The more we pay attention to how we feel, the more connected we are to our most reliable guidance.

connected we are to our most reliable guidance.[1] Are you feeling desperate, lonely, angry, depressed, or frustrated? These are rarely welcome experiences, but they are essential indicators and powerful teachers. When we ignore, deny, or suppress these feelings, we are actually cutting ourselves off from our guidance. We deny our very humanity and our greatest resource.

Think of your emotional life like the gas gauge in your car. When fuel is low, we don't deny it, judge it, or try to control it; we simply acknowledge what it tells us and take the appropriate action to address it. Our feelings are the most reliable gauge of how aligned we are with our true nature, our inner being, or the One Voice; they will guide us back to what we want and away from what we don't.

Our nervous system uses the same basic mechanism—a guidance system comprised of nerves designed to direct us away from pain and toward pleasure. When I touch a hot stove, my nerves don't punish me or judge me, nor do they fire off pain or pleasure for no reason at all. They guide me. They say, "That's probably not where you want to put your hand." I am still given the choice to ignore the guidance if I want.

Our emotional life functions in a similar way. It will give signals and indicators that tell us we are getting more of what we want or less of what we want. Are we full of love, hope, gratitude, appreciation, and excitement? If so, this may be an indication that we are on track. That doesn't mean positive feelings *always* indicate we are listening to the One Voice. Some forms of happiness are superficial distractions designed to assist our denial. Both outcomes are possible. What matters is that we pay attention to our feelings and stay curious about what they might be telling us. Our emotions function a bit like the game I play with my kids when they hide something for me to find. When I get closer, they say, "Warmer," and when I step away from it, they say, "Colder." As I attend to their words and adjust my position accordingly, I'm able to get closer to what I'm after.

The emotional life can be thought of as "warmer" and "colder" feeling states. The Universe gave us an emotional guidance system that constantly whispers, and sometimes shouts, "You're getting closer," or "Now you're farther away." Pay attention to this. The more we listen for and act on this guidance, the more sensitive we become to the smallest prompting of the One Voice. And the sooner we attend to our feeling states, the more our life begins to flow. The struggle begins to ease up as we enter a state of allowing and surrendering.

> *Our negative, or "lower," emotions are as important as our positive, or "higher," emotions.*

To be clear, our negative, or "lower," emotions are as important as our positive, or "higher," emotions. They are both forms of guidance; learning to attend to and appreciate the message of both is essential to this path. As we listen and attend to both, we will learn to awaken our courage and follow our true joy. This is the beginning of the way.

THE SOUND INSIDE

The street artist in a ball cap and jeans drew his bow across his violin, and notes echoed through the busy subway station. For nearly an hour he offered a feast for the ears amid the ant trails that form during morning rush hour in one of the busiest stations in Washington, D.C. More than a thousand people passed by him, without even a glance or acknowledgment of his presence. Fewer than ten people bothered to stop and listen, and even fewer gave money. During that session he made just over thirty-two dollars. The whole thing was captured on a security camera.

Fortunately, the artist also had a day job to help pay the bills. This was Joshua Bell, a man considered one of the world's greatest violinists. He plays in renowned concert halls to sold-out crowds. In concert he earns about a thousand dollars a minute. His instrument of choice: a Stradivarius violin crafted in 1712, worth an estimated $3.5 million.

His foray into the subway was part of an experiment devised and executed by the *Washington Post*.[2] The question in mind: Would people be able to recognize the talent and breathtaking beauty of this artist's performance, and the most enduring music the world has known, in an unexpected context? Would the transcendent music, the priceless instrument, and the virtuoso wielding it be enough to reach through the mundane and make unsuspecting passersby take notice? The answer, it seems, was no.

The people who walked through that subway did not recognize what was in their midst. Their ears were not attuned to the brilliance of the artist, the music, or the instrument. One reason is likely related to expectation and context. The context of a subway station during rush hour is one of mindless repetition, a kind of groove-worn automatic exercise that unfolds with patterned predictability. The other reason may have to do with a lack of familiarity. Most passersby might not have known who Joshua Bell is.

Whatever the reason, the world's greatest violinist was reduced to little more than elevator music as background to busy lives.

The story of Joshua Bell in the subway is the same as what I have seen happen in my life and in the lives of others. Inside all of us, a song plays, a song that may issue forth the most astonishing music the world has known, on the most brilliant and powerful instruments ever made. The problem is, most of us don't recognize it. The instrument is the human heart, the song is the One Voice, and the artist is you.

In order to live in alignment with our purpose, we must become aware of the song of the heart. Let me be clear: when I use the word *heart*, I am not talking about quaint romance or soft sentimental feelings. The heart is the seat of our identity, our deepest desire, and the engine of our purpose and potential. If you want to know yourself, you must know what you want. Desire determines our identity. The heart is also the source of our courage, strength, and power, which we need most to live our purpose. The heart produces the most extraordinary song you will ever hear, a song written and performed by you and for you. No one else will hear it like you will. When you do, make yourself a slave to that rhythm. Let it move you, and you will never be led astray.

In order to live in alignment with our purpose, we must become aware of the song of the heart.

The difference between a great violinist and the *greatest* violinist is apparent only to true connoisseurs, those with an experienced ear. The differences between a cubic zirconium stone and a diamond are apparent only to the practiced and trained eye of a gemologist. We must become connoisseurs of the sound our heart makes. Sometimes this is obvious, but most of the time it is subtle and requires practice. We get good at what we practice. The more we are attentive to the voice of the heart, the simpler our decision making becomes. But this isn't just about making "good" decisions and avoiding "bad" ones. It is about making choices that align with the rudder of our being rather than living at odds with it.

The heart will not often promote itself with billboards, spectacle, and flashing lights. It will humbly and persistently show up in every corner of life, in the most unexpected ways or places, intending to be heard. Fortunately for us, it does not take kindly to being ignored. In time, symptoms that indicate we are deaf to its song will show up. Sleepless nights, fatigue, overeating, overexercising, boredom, depression, and anxiety can be signs that our deepest intuitions, instincts, and desires are being ignored. Once again, our guidance system never fails us.

In order to notice the song on this incredible

instrument, we must become attentive and practiced in the ways of the inner life. Some of the techniques and practices will be outlined in the following chapters.

Practice develops strength, even expertise. However, we should always work to retain a beginner's mind in this process. Experts are at risk of becoming calcified from years of learning in a closed and tidy system of assumptions, which leaves little room for new learning and new possibilities, assumptions, and realities. A perpetual student, however, remains open to new levels of reality and fresh possibilities. She retains a deep sense of anticipation, curiosity, and attentiveness. Assume this posture and you can unleash the courage to create the life you most desire and activate your great potential.

3

DOES WHAT I WANT MATTER?

A once neatly coiled green extension cord now lay in a tangled pile at the feet of my seven-year-old daughter and her friend. They had hauled it out from the garage and were making efforts to tie a knot and a loop at one end. It seemed an unusual accessory for kids to play with, so I popped my head out the front door and asked what they were doing. "We're playing cowboys, and this is our rope. We found it in the garage. We're making a lasso to save people from hot lava," she said, pointing in the general direction of the sidewalk, which was now a river of molten magma.

I allowed it but decided to supervise their activity from afar. Before long, to my surprise, they had something that resembled a lasso in hand. It was cumbersome and too heavy, but it worked—sort of. They took turns saving imaginary friends from the lava river. Eventually they laid it out across the sidewalk and began using it as a tightrope to traverse the treacherous hazard.

An extension cord is not the best medium for a lasso; a rope is much better. Nonetheless they made it work. Of course, it was a vast underutilization of the true power of an extension cord. This conduit, which channels electric energy, appeared as mundane as a rope to them. Yet it is a very powerful technology. Little did they know what they held in their hands, nor did they much care.

As it turns out, you can use an extension cord as a rope and it works pretty well, but it hardly leverages the true potential. A teacher of mine likes to say, "You can use a flute to stir soup and it will work just fine, but that is not what it is made for." The same is true when it comes to people. A person can do a lot of things, but that doesn't mean he was made for them. What we *can do* and what we were *made for* are not the same. Understanding and living this distinction is an important aspect to living our purpose.

> *"You can use a flute to stir soup and it will work just fine, but that is not what it is made for."*

Valerie sat across from me with a look of frustration. The church where I served as pastor had recently hired her as a bookkeeper. We were a small community rapidly growing and in need of more professional services. Prior to her coming on board, our finances were handled in an informal way through a rotating cadre of well-meaning but sometimes unskilled volunteers. Bookkeeping was Valerie's trade, and she came with an impeccable reputation. She applied her considerable attention to detail, proactivity, organizational acumen, and a command of IRS code to our books. She did a lot of cleaning up, and it was a huge help. Her contribution was even noticed by members of the community. She instilled such confidence that we started noticing an increase in giving patterns. People found our community deserving of money, which they felt would be well handled now.

Valerie was also a member of our community, but on this day she sat in my office as a parishioner, not an employee. I was talking to her about the amazing impact her contribution was having. While she was glad to hear it, her frustration was mounting. When I asked her what the trouble was, she said, "I know I'm good at this stuff, but I don't really like doing it. Why couldn't I be good at something more interesting?" It was a fascinating question. This was not a question of value or contribution. It was a question of her enjoyment, engagement, and, ultimately, desire.

At some point in life many of us will try out a skill and receive positive feedback. We may even get offered considerable money for that skill. We may notice we do it better than others. Often that compels us to keep doing it. We may persist for a season, but eventually nascent questions we have forgotten will emerge: *Do I like this? Is this what I want to do?*

I know others like what I do for them, but does it matter that I don't like doing it? Many of us neglect to consider these simple but crucial questions.

WHAT DO YOU WANT?

The difference between what we *can do* and what we are *made for* is found in our desire. If you want to know what you were made for, then you have to answer the questions *What do you want?* and *What excites you most?* These are the most overlooked and important questions we must answer in order to live with direction, clarity, and purpose.

> *The difference between what we can do and what we are made for is found in our desire.*

The flute stirring soup may be effective, even helpful, but it is underutilized and unhappy. Its gift to the world is lost. When we use a flute for its intended purpose of playing music, something beautiful is unleashed. To live our purpose, we first have to know what we want. If we don't, many others will gladly choose it for us. The One Voice is always speaking our deepest desires. The challenge is to listen for it and have the courage to act once we hear it.

Knowing what you want is a process of

clarifying, getting more refined and more specific over time and through experience. Negative experiences are very useful to us. They serve an important function; mostly they clarify what we actually want. In a negative experience we get a dose of what we don't want, which helps us see what we do want. So knowing what we don't want is helpful. However, this is not a process of elimination—at some point we must focus our attention on what we *do* want rather than what we don't. This is a crucial step. The reason is that our focus of attention will make all the difference in the outcome.

The mountains of the Sonoran Desert are a stunning but unforgiving terrain complete with jagged rocks, steep cliffs, and saguaros. I live just minutes from a desert preserve—a haven for mountain bikers. When I first moved there years ago, I made a concerted effort to take up this activity more seriously. As a thirtysomething at the time, I had a growing awareness of my responsibilities to my family and my mortality. Mountain biking was both thrilling and liberating, but early on I white-knuckled my way down the mountain, body tense, eyes scanning the path ahead for rocks and ledges I needed to avoid. Somehow my bike was a magnet for rocks, often resulting in a crash, a flat tire, or an additional premature gray hair.

One day I was riding with a friend who was a

seasoned mountain biker. My frustration, fear, and lack of skill were evident and slowing us down. He was both patient and kind enough to offer some advice.

"When you're going down the mountain," he said, "whatever you do, don't look at the object you want to avoid. You will hit it every time. Instead, look where you want to go. The biomechanics of your body will naturally align the bike wherever you look. I know it sounds weird, but it works. Also, make sure you keep your arms loose; you seem really tense on the bike. The more flexible your body is, the more likely you will weather the bumps. Think of yourself like water flowing down a mountain, able to adapt effortlessly and easily."

I got on the bike again and did as he told me. At first it felt terrifying and unnatural. We approached a familiar section of the path populated by a series of ill-placed rocks forming a narrow and treacherous route. I had never made it through unscathed before. This time I did as he instructed and allowed myself to look only to the place on the path I wanted to go. The rocks faded into my periphery. I loosened my grip on the handlebars and relaxed my arms. Like magic, my bike easily threaded the needle and rolled through the narrow pass without any trouble. I couldn't believe how simple it was. It worked just as he described. I had hit dozens of rocks in previous attempts. This time, it was as though they had disappeared.

The rule I learned while mountain biking points to a larger principle in life: *energy follows attention.* By placing our attention on what we want, rather than on what we don't want, we unconsciously and automatically recruit resources to align around our attention. In a very real sense we get more of what we focus on.

> ***The rule I learned while mountain biking points to a larger principle in life: energy follows attention.***

The equation is simple: Focus on what you don't want, and more of it will come. Focus on what you do want and more of it will come.

This is quite possibly the most important lesson to learn when it comes to living the life you want. It cannot be overstated that we live in a universe where we get what we focus on. It may not be instantaneous, but give it time and you will accumulate and draw whatever your attention is on. Focus on the feeling that people don't like you and you don't have friends, and guess what? Over time, people will not want anything to do with you. Fixate on how much debt you have and how little income you have and how there's no hope of that ever changing, and over time things will get worse. Focus on how much you appreciate your spouse and all the wonderful things about him or her, and those things will be drawn forth and become amplified. Because this cause and effect happens slowly, it's difficult to make the connection. That's why my mountain biking lesson was so instructive. It showed me in real time the simple fact that energy follows attention.

As an experiment, choose one part of your life that is mildly annoying, but nothing too big. For a few minutes once or twice a day for ten straight days focus only on the most positive aspects of that annoying part of your life. Write down the things you appreciate about it. If they're too difficult to find, pick something more general. After the ten days, notice what changes have occurred since you started the exercise. (Ten is not a magic number; the changes may happen much sooner, but something will shift.)

The second piece of advice my friend gave me that day is also insightful: stay flexible. Life is unpredictable; the path is usually not well marked and presents many unexpected turns and obstacles. Our ability to respond and correct our course in the face of changes and barriers is crucial to our success. The more flexible and adaptable we are to the terrain, the more likely we

Our ability to respond and correct our course in the face of changes and barriers is crucial to our success.

are to get down the mountain with ease and enjoyment. Another way to say it is that my body became receptive to changing conditions. It was available for course correction without planning or effort. I was moving too fast, and there were too many moving parts in that moment for me to plot with precision and control my course through the obstacles. It required a kind of allowing, more than effort.

The discipline of focusing on what you want and a posture of relaxed allowing are two of the most crucial practices in living our highest potential and deepest purpose.

OUT OF THE SHADOWS

The first step in doing the work of listening for the One Voice is to remove all judgment and fear. Nonjudging acceptance is necessary to facilitate the most critical ingredient of knowing what you want: honesty. We must be willing to tell ourselves the truth. We must honestly admit to ourselves what we want. Our beliefs often prevent this because we use them to apply a lens of judgment to our desires. We may have been taught to believe some desires are good, and others are bad. Undoubtedly, acting on certain desires will make life a lot more complex and difficult. However, judging a desire prematurely short-circuits the process of uncovering our deepest desires. If you label a desire for more money, fame, or even something like revenge as "bad," "selfish," or "dark," you will be encouraged to hide that desire from yourself. It moves into the unconscious realm. However, just because you can't see it anymore doesn't mean it has gone away. In fact, it often gains more steam and grows stronger in the shadows.

To help alleviate the judgment of a desire, it helps to remember that there is a difference between a desire and a decision. A desire is a feeling; a decision is an action. Every desire, no matter how dark it may seem, is instructive and offers guidance of some kind. Every desire, no matter what, is a valid and important guide or teacher on the path of purpose. Beneath and behind each desire is likely a positive intention. Beneath a desire to get even or exact vengeance is a desire for balance and equality. Behind the desire for fame and recognition may be a desire to feel worthy and appreciated. Beneath the desire for power is a longing for freedom and choices. Notice that some desires you may deem as less noble, or even "dark," still point to something very important.

Every desire, no matter what, is a valid and important guide or teacher on the path.

When judgment is released, light shines and our path is made known. When desire comes out of the shadows, you connect with your guidance. However, this does not mean we must act on every desire.

Knowing this difference allows us to explore desires without dismissing or suppressing them out of fear. What we may judge to be dark, childish, dangerous, or unrealistic is often the carrier of hidden clues to our path. Learning to welcome and befriend all our desires and emotions is crucial. When we let our desires into the light, we can truly assess what they have to say and how we can express them to serve us and others best.

This process is designed to unveil the deeper, more truthful desires. I learned early on in life how to disguise my desires from myself without knowing it. This little habit has remained with me throughout life. It caused a tremendous cloud of confusion many times both personally and professionally. Until I was able to risk honesty, first with myself even in little things, I could not get in touch with my guidance system. I struggled to find the clarity I was looking for. The reason for my self-deception had everything to do with my desire to win the approval of others. I simply learned to mirror and adapt like a chameleon to what others wanted and needed. I learned to want what others wanted me to want.

One of my earliest memories of this is when

I was in fifth grade. I was with an older kid, a seventh grader, on the playground after school. He pulled out a can of dipping tobacco, showed me how to put a dip in, and told me not to swallow. I did as he said and discovered the taste was so revolting I nearly threw up. He looked at me and said, "Isn't it awesome?" I thought he was from another planet. I looked him dead in the eyes and said, "I love it!" and kept it in as long as I could take it. This is a common story of peer pressure. But my personality remained susceptible to this way of living long past the time it should have. I simply lied in order to be liked. It didn't matter that I was pretending to be someone I wasn't. I had won his approval. This is one of the more dangerous and common patterns that will prevent a person from living his purpose and hearing the One Voice.

The more suppressed or out of touch we are with our desires, the more distorted and convoluted the process will become. As someone well acquainted with pretending not to want, I have experienced this fog on more than one occasion. This was most evident when I made the unexpected transition from working in advertising to serving as a pastor.

I enjoyed advertising, I liked the perks of the job and wanted to keep doing it. But something in me was restless. I didn't have words to describe what was happening, or any rationale for my restlessness, but I knew I had to do something about it. It was related to meaning. I didn't feel the significance I wanted to feel in that line of work.

I had an immediate aversion to the thought of becoming a pastor, a notion that oddly entered my head many times and that others told me I should consider. It was a strong and visceral reaction I didn't understand. I didn't *want* that. I wanted something else; I just didn't know what it was.

Through a series of practices (outlined in the next chapter) a strange thing happened. I learned the one thing I thought I didn't want was actually what I wanted most. This wasn't about a job so much as a way of contributing in the world. This desire was not apparent to me; it was covered over. I had repressed it out of fear. I was afraid it wasn't possible to find work that was meaningful for me. It is possible to train ourselves out of a conscious desire for something if we are utterly convinced it is impossible. If we assume something is impossible, the desire for it may be too painful, and so we suppress it. Fears, both conscious and unconscious, can be a powerful force that drives the One Voice underground. As a result, we may run from

Fears, both conscious and unconscious, can be a powerful force that drives the One Voice underground.

or make choices that take us away from the path that beckons us. The good news is that the desire will not abandon us even if we seek to abandon it. At some point, it returns.

Fear is not the only force to aid denial. We keep subterranean desires under wraps when we numb out with things like watching TV, using social media, surfing the web, reading, drinking, or indulging in other leisure activities and surface pleasures. The problem is not with these things in and of themselves. Instead, it's how they come to function in our lives. Any of these can serve as white noise that drowns out the One Voice—a deeper desire.

Not long ago I was on a vacation where I allowed myself to eat whatever I wanted. No restrictions. I enjoyed a wide range of decadent foods, all of which were light on nutrition and calorie dense. It was bliss. After three or four days, my taste buds had still not tired of this regimen. They would have gladly continued to enjoy more of the same. But I just couldn't keep eating like that; my body was craving nutrient-rich foods. I began searching out foods I typically don't long for—dark-green vegetables. It was as though my body was overriding the preferences of my palate. When I responded and started eating more sensibly, I felt greater vitality and resilience.

When it comes to food, there are two levels

on which cravings can function. One is the level of the palate; the other is deeper and related to the needs of the body. Pregnant woman are often quite familiar with this strange experience. Sometimes the pleasures from our taste buds are at odds with the optimum functioning of the body. The palate wants flavors; the body desires nutrients.

For me advertising served as a desire at the level of my palate, but this was not my deepest desire. My decision to leave advertising and enter the process of becoming a pastor functioned at the level of a soul craving. This was not something I longed for on the surface. I was busy being governed by the pleasures of my palate. It was only when I took the time to pay attention to the deep places in me that I could feel the buried longing that revealed more of what I was made for.

4

HOW DO I FIND WHAT I WANT MOST?

I'm not doing very well," John mumbled. One half of his body and part of his head were wrapped in various casts and gauze, with metal rods and hardware protruding. As he lay in the hospital bed, I felt deep sympathy and was full of questions. No one really knows the stories before walking in the room. His words were expected, given his serious condition, but what he said next was not.

"I'm just really disappointed," he said.

"What disappoints you the most?" I asked.

"I'm still alive."

Silence was the only appropriate response, but I knew I had to be a big enough presence to take the information without betraying my shock. John was twenty-five years old and looked like a kid to me. As we talked, I learned that John had thrown himself from a fourth-story window in an attempted suicide but had miraculously survived. I listened as he shared all the reasons he no longer wanted to live. We sat together for a while, and I listened as he talked. With people in this condition, I've learned to offer presence and acceptance and to enter their world. Any attempt to argue John back into life was a bridge too far in his state. That would be for another day.

The job was like that. I would walk into a room with no clue what I was getting into. I knew their stories would involve some kind of trauma and tragedy, but that's all. Some didn't want to talk, or couldn't. But most wanted me to stay. They looked to me for comfort, wisdom, and healing. They wanted something, anything, to help them cope with a life that had been scrambled like an egg.

During my internship as a hospital chaplain at UCLA Medical Center I learned about the hidden power of the inner life. Two weeks into the program I found myself utterly spent. That day I had visited with only two patients, the visits lasting a little less than an hour and a half. One was a fifty-year-old Russian woman who had been shot multiple times in an alley mugging and survived. She was having intense nightmares and struggling to make sense of the trauma, to say nothing of the physical pain she was enduring. The other patient was John in the room next door. I stayed present and listened to them. Not much can be said. I made a few observations, and a suggestion or two for how to adjust to their new reality, but mostly I felt completely out of my depth.

I was done for the day and it wasn't even 10:00 a.m. *What is wrong with me?* I thought. I was there to work an eight-hour day; I should have been able to see at least a dozen people. But the thought was unfathomable. That day I learned the job required a very specific skill I didn't have—access to powerful inner resources and personal boundaries. Without these I soaked up every ounce of physical, emotional, and psychological suffering and carried it with me for the day. It was as if I had an empty bucket that each patient would fill to the brim with their pain. Then I would carry it to the next room not knowing how to empty it after each visit and let it go. The more seasoned chaplains had learned this unusual skill. They were deeply practiced in the ways of the inner life and had cultivated a capacity to connect completely without allowing the suffering to stick to them.

The more seasoned chaplains had learned this unusual skill. They were deeply practiced in the ways of the inner life.

Sandi, the head of the chaplaincy program, was a tall, gray-haired woman, with gravitas who had been a chaplain for many years. I noticed early on that she seemed to have a kind of regular access to certain internal resources. Somehow over the years she had developed an ability to withstand the incredible emotional hazards of this job.

One day as we were talking, I began to share some of my frustrations with the job as well as my broader concern around finding my purpose. I was trying different things, a chaplaincy among them, but I still felt like I was coming up empty-handed. I shared my many efforts and attempts to figure it out. She listened intently; then, after a moment, she reached into her desk drawer, pulled out a sticky note, and began writing. Without looking up she said, "You need Judith," and handed me the paper with a phone number.

"She's retired now from this kind of work, but mention my name and she might meet with you. She will teach you to sit and be quiet." The words may have sounded like a schoolteacher's scolding, but her tone was far more eager than punitive, as if she knew the contents of a gift I was about to open.

I didn't understand what she meant, but I was very curious and figured I didn't have anything to lose. When I made the call, a serene and gentle voice answered.

"Hello, this is Judith."

"Hi, Judith. My name is Shane Hipps. Sandi gave me your number and said you might be able to help me. Do you have a minute to talk?" I was trying to affect a confident, likable, and not-too-needy-but-just-in-need-enough tone of voice. I shared with her my situation, my search, and my frustration at not being able to figure out what I wanted to do with my life. After I finished, there was a long pause.

"Yes... I can hear the urgency in your

questions," she said. "But I don't do this work anymore. I'm retired."

I was a little disappointed though not surprised. Sandi had warned me this was a possibility.

"But I'm intrigued," she continued. "I'm not sure why but I'm getting the sense I should sit with this before deciding. Would it be OK if I called you back in two days with my decision?"

"Of course," I replied.

Time moved through molasses over the next two days. I didn't know much about this woman, but I knew I really wanted to meet with her. After two days, the phone rang.

"Shane, this is Judith."

My heart rate quickened. I cleared my throat, trying not to betray my anxiety. In a cool, overconfident, and detached voice I answered. "Hey, Judith. How are you?"

"I'm well, thanks."

My anxiety surprised me. I didn't realize how much I wanted her to say yes, how much I needed her help. More was riding on her answer than I had let myself admit until that moment. I braced for what came next.

"I just wanted to call you back as we agreed," she said. "Is now a good time to talk?"

"Yes," I said.

"As you know, I wanted to sit with your request

before deciding, and I did just that. At first my response was that I'm retired and would be unable to meet. But over the two days a different answer emerged. So, I would be willing to take one meeting with you for an hour. After that, each of us can decide if we should continue meeting. Does that sound like something you'd be interested in?"

I jumped at the chance. Our first meeting was strange and wonderful. By the end of it I felt I had only scratched the surface of something very important, but I didn't know what. I was desperately hoping she would agree to meet again. To my great relief, she decided to continue meeting with me.

I ended up spending a year with Judith. During our many times together she introduced me to unusual practices. She would greet me at the door and hug me. Her embrace carried depth, almost as if information was being transmitted physically. It was grounding. I also had the sense she was reading my body intuitively. Then she would ask me to sit. Each session began the same way. We were to sit in silence together for as long as necessary. Then I would speak out of the silence when I was ready. It was always up to me to break the silence whenever I was ready with whatever I wanted to say. No other instructions were given. I had been to see mentors, and a therapist or two, but this was very different.

In the early days, the silence was very awkward.

I never knew what I was supposed to think or do during that time. My mind was mostly scattered, confused, a little scared, and trying to come up with something interesting to say to start the conversation. The silence would last maybe a minute if I was lucky, and then I needed to say something to get out of the silence. She never indicated if this was good or bad.

Over time, I noticed that the silence, while unusual, was no longer awkward. In fact, it got much easier even after the first two visits—the minutes would tick by and I barely noticed the time anymore. I began to pay attention to the quality of the moment, the currents of my emotions, thoughts, and energy inside. She had given me instructions to start practicing silence on my own. I noticed that when I was with her, she functioned like an energetic anchor. Silence was much easier with her than with just me. She had practiced this kind of silence for decades. Being with her changed the quality of my practice; she had a grounding effect on me, almost as if the method I learned were something caught, not taught. Her presence allowed me to experience the silence more deeply. Soon I learned the value of sitting and being quiet, just as Sandi had predicted.

Over several months at home and with Judith I began to experience an opening within me that I didn't know existed. Through the practice of silence and solitude I learned how to awaken a connection to a deeper place, one that felt like the eye of a hurricane—a place of calm and stillness in the midst of chaos swirling around. Each time I would arrive as a wound-up ball of stress, feeling overwhelmed by the demands of life and an unknown future. Each time I would leave in a state of peace even though everything in my life was exactly the same as when I had arrived. What changed was not the happenings in my life but my relationship to my life. She did not give much advice, only direction to finding the source of answers inside.

> *What changed was not the happenings in my life but my relationship to my life.*

This newfound habit of centering in stillness opened a door within. I began to hear myself more clearly. I began to learn how to sift through the subtle sounds of the counterfeit voices in order to hear the One Voice within. Soon, the sense of desire became clearer.

LEARNING TO SIT AND BE QUIET

The human experience immerses us in a sea of desires. Some are biologically determined, others are passing whims, and still others may be addictions or compulsions. Sometimes our desires may appear at odds with each other. I may want to make more money but also spend more time with my family. These two desires will appear to require negotiation or trade-off.

For some the answer to the question *What do I want?* is obvious. However, getting to the true heart of our deepest desire is not always as simple as it seems. Desire is a feeling, and feelings move and change constantly. How do you see a reflection in water clearly? The water must be perfectly still. The surface of a lake, exposed to the elements, is rarely still. Surface feelings are like that, too. They move and are bandied about by the elements, the whims of others, and the conditions of life. But when you learn to descend into the depths, the water becomes increasingly still, untouched by the elements. From here clarity can begin to emerge.

Desires are often stacked with the deeper ones hidden from view until we clear away the ones on top. The surface desires are not less valid or worse than the deeper ones. Their horizon is simply shorter; they tend to be more passing. But the deeper ones have a tendency to be more abiding and immovable.

Several techniques can be helpful in sifting through multiple voices to find the one we are looking for. These techniques all begin with a practice that helps us pay attention to the present moment. The reason is simple. In reality, the past and the future don't actually exist; they are merely memory or imagination, figment or fantasy. The moment

The techniques described here work best when we find stillness inside first.

called "now" is the only place that is real. The one place we find the One Voice is in this moment. The techniques described here work best when we find stillness inside first.

If you have a practice of meditation, silent centering prayer, or something like it, use that. If not, I've listed two preparation practices designed to ground you in the present. Take as long as you want, but if you're impatient or short on time, it takes only a few minutes.

Centering Option #1: The Body Scan

The mind has little access to the present moment. It spends most of its time revisiting the past or fantasizing about the future. The closest it can get to the present is one millisecond behind when it narrates the moment. The body, however, exists only in the present. It cannot reside in the past or the future. As a result, the body is a perfect conductor that guides our attention and awareness to the here and now. It carries a vast amount of untapped wisdom. This is our only vehicle to carry us through life. We get only one, and yet it is easily and often forgotten.

To begin, sit comfortably, close your eyes, breathe naturally, and turn your attention to your body. Notice your feet on the floor, your legs, pelvis, genitals, belly, chest, arms, shoulders, neck, jaw, and face. Pause briefly on each body part. Pay attention to any parts you are more aware of than others. Notice any sensations, pains, numbness, or tensions that exist. Note them briefly and move on. The body is always communicating; it is a feeling machine. Let it speak for a few minutes. When you feel relatively centered in the present, open your eyes, choose one of the techniques below, and follow the instructions.

Centering Option #2: Breath Work

If you prefer a different centering practice before you engage the techniques below, consider this one. Between our first inhale and our last exhale lies our existence. Breath is the one mathematical and immovable constant in our life. No matter what happens in life, breath is always bringing us the gift of existence. Our breath comes only in the moment called now. We cannot store it up or give it away. Focusing our attention here can help us come to this moment.

To begin, sit comfortably, close your eyes, and pay attention to the sensation of the breath entering just beneath your nose. Follow the inhale down into your chest and belly, and trace the exhale out through your nose. Notice the rhythmic expansion and contraction of your torso as life fills you. Remember that this perpetual swing is the only thing that separates us from the dirt outside. After a few moments of paying attention to your breath, open your eyes, choose one of the techniques below, and follow the instructions.

THE "LITTLE THINGS" TECHNIQUE

Consider the possibility that your joy, bliss, and excitement are essential to living your purpose. Your joy is not only the engine in your car, but also your navigation system. Remove it and you will be lost and no longer moving. It's important that we slow down for a moment and allow ourselves to explore desire, the stuff that gives us a high, the things that we enjoy no matter how mundane and insignificant we judge them to be. The object of the desire is less important than the desire itself. Much of this path is an exercise in trust and suspended judgment. It means releasing control and manipulation. It means turning over all the mechanisms to a power much greater and more loving than we can imagine.

> *Your joy is not only the engine in your car, but also your navigation system.*

Choose the smallest thing in this moment that you prefer to do. It could be to keep reading this book, take a warm bath, eat some food, watch a movie, get some work done, meet up with a friend, or exercise. Whatever it is, just follow it. Your attention is not on any particular outcome, just a feeling that says, "Yes, I like this." That's all you are after in this experiment.

Once you've acted on that choice to the best of your ability and have taken it as far as you want, notice what happens to your desire. Where does it go next? Did it go toward a nap, or a walk outside, or planning a trip? Start here in the smallest places. Nothing is mundane. The desire that leads to these small choices is the same mechanism that leads us through much larger ones. The bigger ones are not better or more significant; they just come with more fear and more limiting beliefs. And therefore they have a tendency to lock up in us. Start small every day, noticing your level of interest and excitement, and then follow it. Use this practice for one week. Every day, several times a day, notice what you want in the little things. Allow that muscle of attending to the subtle shifts in desire to strengthen. Once you have the hang of it, this will serve as your most important resource for finding your desires in the larger choices.

The desire that leads to these small choices is the same mechanism that leads us through much larger ones.

THE "TEN-YEAR-OLD" TECHNIQUE

Before counterfeit voices have entered our awareness, before the mind has developed elaborate maps of the world, and before our worldviews and beliefs limit us, we enter this world with a directive, a DNA birthright that comes in the form of desire. We are closer to the simple desires of the heart. Before belonging needs and the wishes of others crowd out our desires, we are more naturally in touch with innate clarity. When we feel particularly adrift in life, unsure of where we are headed or what we are here to do, sometimes revisiting the wishes of our childhood reveal important clues. Reflecting on the meaning of your childhood interests is a bit like interpreting a dream. The memory and meaning are not always immediate or obvious, but the exercise can be quite illuminating.

As a child, I always wanted to be an architect. I enjoyed spending time designing and drafting elaborate buildings, most of which defied the laws of physics. As I got older, I learned that architecture required robust training and proficiency in mathematics, a subject I had neither an interest in nor aptitude for. My interest in architecture faded and I moved on to other things. As I reflect on this childhood wish, I can see the antecedents for one aspect of my purpose in the world. Today I seek to understand and arrange different concepts and ideas to create new possibilities and ways of seeing the world. In this way I am very much an architect, not of physical structures, but of ideas and relationships.

Think back to your childhood. Do you remember how you answered the question *What do you want to be when you grow up?* If so, what specifically captured your interest in the occupation you chose? In what ways have you found yourself engaged in pursuits that harken back to that interest? Pay careful attention to things you may think are insignificant or unrealistic. These are often important clues to your purpose.

Pay careful attention to things you may think are insignificant or unrealistic.

If you have difficulty remembering and are willing to try something unusual, sit down and write a dialogue with your ten-year-old self. Literally imagine meeting up with the ten-year-old you wherever he or she most likes to be. And ask yourself a few questions. Things like, *What do you like to do? What excites you? What do you imagine doing when you grow up?* Then record the answers that come to you. Don't worry about remembering something accurately; let that part of you speak now, and accept whatever comes up. You may be surprised by what you learn. This is one way to access the part of you that still exists but that you have forgotten, learned to invalidate, or ignored. The ten-year-old has a great deal of truth to offer.

THE "IF I DIED TOMORROW" TECHNIQUE

Sometimes dramatic experiences are a powerful force in clarifying what matters. In a sense, they can temporarily turn off the white noise of life. The clarity of what matters most to us comes into full relief when we lose a loved one, face serious illness, or experience a major loss. Death is a persuasive teacher. At some point, we all face this prospect. However, true wisdom is the ability to see clearly before tragedy hits, the ability to wake up before the alarm jolts us awake.

In this experiment begin by surveying the way you spend your time, whom you spend it with, how you use your skills, and what contributions you make in the world. Then ask yourself, *If I died tomorrow, would I have lived doing what I was made for?* If your answer is yes, then congratulations. You're on the right track. If the answer is no, then consider why this is. Are you taking the necessary steps to get where you need to be? Are you stalled out and aimless? Or are you on the

> *Ask yourself, If I died tomorrow, would I have lived doing what I was made for?*

wrong path entirely? This technique is intended to help us review and if necessary upset or reset our priorities before a crisis forces us to do so. Often an insight can show us whether a course correction is necessary and what we're really after in life.

THE "SELF-INQUIRY" TECHNIQUE

For this technique a journal of some kind can be helpful. A nonjudging and trusted friend or guide can also perform it verbally with you if you prefer. After you have found your way into the moment by using a method of your choosing or a practice from above, write down at the top of the page the question *What do I want?* Ask yourself the question and write down the answer. Don't think about it too much; just record the first thing that comes up. It could be banal, mundane, or even immoral. Judgments of any kind are not helpful at this point; they only reinforce denial. Write down the answer. Then after a brief pause ask the question again. Write the next thing that comes up; it could be existential, biological, or emotional. Continue this process for about twenty or thirty minutes.

You may feel you have exhausted your answers in the first five minutes. However, do not assume that you have only one deep desire. Imagine it as the layers of an onion; in peeling away each layer, you get closer to the next one. Be patient and expectant. With each new layer you may need to stay awhile until the heart is ready to issue the next one. Often the question mines deep places in us that have long been covered over, ignored, or even repressed. Keep going. Don't worry about repeated desires; just keep asking and answering until you have completed the time frame.

The next step requires a kind of indifference. We are looking to maintain a posture of openness and acceptance. In other words, we seek to remove preconceptions and judgments. Take a moment and *release what others want you to want, and what you want to want.* Divest yourself of outcomes so you can see clearly what the deepest part of you might be saying.

> *Take a moment and release what others want you to want, and what you want to want.*

Once you are there, look over the list of things you have written down. As you scan the desires, mark the ones that seem to have the most energy around them. Use your intuition to guide what you should pay attention to. Notice what themes seem to repeat. This technique is one of the best for those who are feeling stuck and unclear about what they are here for, or which step to take next. It is not a silver bullet or a worked-out plan. Instead, this exercise usually provides just enough light on the next step of the path.

THE "IF I WASN'T AFRAID" TECHNIQUE

Fear is a helpful emotion; it's an important guide that protects us from danger. Fear resulting from seeing a snake, or a shark in the water, is useful. However, if the fear persists long after you are safely at home, it becomes a problem. Often our fears are born of threats that are imagined. Fear can cause us to distort our reality. In the process it can also evoke experiences that wouldn't otherwise happen. *Energy follows attention.* In other words, we get what we focus on, even when it's something we don't want. Fear is one of the great obstacles to being who we are. Living and creating the life we want takes more than just finding and following our desire. It requires courage. Clearing away the fear.

Living and creating the life we want takes more than just finding and following our desire. It requires courage.

In this technique, simply complete this statement: *If I wasn't afraid, I would...* Begin by centering yourself, and answer this question in regard to different areas of your life. For relationships, complete this question: *If I wasn't afraid in my marriage, I would...* You may also ask the question about your professional, social, or financial life. The answers may surprise you. Whatever you come up with, consider a small step you could take to act on this desire.

THE "OPPOSITE" TECHNIQUE

Begin by looking at something in your life you are really dissatisfied with. It could be related to your health, your body image, your financial situation, or relationship difficulty. Focus for a moment on what you don't like about it. What is most frustrating, saddening, or difficult about it? As you think about it, begin to write down your answer or say it to yourself. For example, you might say, "I can't stand how boring my job is; I feel trapped." Or, "I'm sick of my spouse always criticizing me." Then as you begin to express it, you may start to feel more negative emotion. As this builds, begin to turn your focus toward the thing you want most. Let your negative emotion become an indicator of what you want most. In other words, you may go from saying, "I can't stand how boring my job is; I feel trapped," to, "I want a job that excites me and feels freeing with a lot of flexibility."

Let your negative emotion become an indicator of what you want most.

Implied in what we don't want is the very thing we do want. Sometimes we forget to convert it and focus our attention there. Taking this technique one step further, you could remember a time in your past when you had the thing you wanted. Revisit that experience and bring the emotional quality of it into the present moment. The event may have happened in the past, but the emotional resource will be suddenly alive in the present. This becomes a helpful companion to guide and allows more of what you're looking for into your life.

Not all of these techniques will interest you. Some will be more powerful and connecting than others. Play with the ones that interest you and ignore the ones that don't. The outcome for each technique is only an indication of which way to go or what might be next, not necessarily an ultimate answer. These are like clues in a treasure hunt, pointing to the next step, not the final one. While a sudden and clear direction is possible, more subtle outcomes can be just as useful. The point here is to find a way to excavate your desires from the deep places within you. Desire is the starting point, but there is another ingredient on the path.

WHAT IS IMPORTANT TO YOU?

In the final year of seminary, after having spent time using the practices noted above, I arrived at an unmistakable desire. I wanted to be a catalyst in people's development and growth. This longing had been with me from the earliest time, but now I had language to describe it. However, finding and naming the truth of our desire is only the beginning. Longings, even when named, are still nebulous. Taking action and concrete steps on vague intuition can be a challenge.

We also need to consider and understand what is important to us. This is a question of *values* or *beliefs*. Values and desires are related but distinct. A value provides a container or boundary condition for our desire. I may *value* the environment, but have a *desire* to tell stories through the arts. That would provide a contour to my purpose that is slightly different from the purpose of someone who *values* the environment but has a *desire* to be in public service. A similar value coupled with a different desire will cause a life path that looks quite different. Our values (what matters most to us or what we believe) provide direction for how best to express our deepest desire. Understanding what matters to us provides important clues for which trail to follow.

> *A value provides a container or boundary condition for our desire.*

Sometimes our values are immediately apparent, straightforward, and easily named—for example, family, equality, art, discipline, adventure, community, excellence, freedom, and efficiency. Other times, an indirect inquiry can uncover hidden values we haven't named or noticed. A brief audit of our time and finances can be quite revealing. How do I spend my time currently? Where would I like to be spending my time? Where do I invest, spend, or give my money? If I had more money, where would I want to invest, spend, or give it? Equally helpful is a survey of your bookshelf or bookmarks on your web browser. What are my intellectual pursuits? What am I reading? What do I find most interesting? A surprising place to uncover our values is by considering what makes us angry. Lurking behind most of our angry responses is a value—something very important to us—that was ignored or violated. Answers to these questions provide data points to help draw out the constellation of our values.

Our desire and our values exist in an ongoing dynamic dance. They are not static. A value might change, while a desire could stay the same, or vice versa. We may always want to tell stories through film, while our value may shift from the environment to generating wealth. Or we may always feel education is very important, but our desire to teach may evolve into a desire to lead in administrative capacities, a desire to do fund-raising, or a desire to help shape public policy. Paying attention to both desire and values is essential on the path of potential and purpose.

When you begin to articulate your values, it is also worth investigating where these beliefs came from. Your beliefs about what's important may be innate, or they may have been borrowed from the people who raised you, from those you want to emulate, or from those you want to avoid. Understanding the origins of your beliefs and the functions they serve will also help you see if any of the beliefs should be updated, developed, or left behind. Beliefs can be a resource or a constraint to our path. A conscious examination of these, as well as the reasons you hold them, can help you hone your quest.

> *Understanding the origins of your beliefs and the functions they serve will also help you see if any of the beliefs should be updated, developed, or left behind.*

WHAT ARE YOU GOOD AT?

Desire and talent, though often confused, are not the same thing. You actually determine each through opposite means. When it comes to your deepest desire, you are the only one who can identify it. No one else can tell you what it is. Others can help you confirm, guide, or give language to that desire, but ultimately it comes from inside you.

When it comes to our aptitude, what we're good at, the opposite is true. The way we know if we're good at something is based on external feedback. You will know you are good at something when people outside you recognize and name it, when your efforts result in an impact or contribution or evoke a response. Whether our aptitude is related to affecting people, understanding and manipulating data, or working with physical things, the external world will keep us informed of our skillfulness.

In seminary I had never given a sermon in my life. I felt relatively at ease speaking in front of people, and speech communication was one of my majors in college. But preaching seemed a very specific kind of art form that deals with deeply personal matters that are important to people. I felt considerable anxiety and pressure when I imagined preaching. During my first class on preaching, where all the students were required to prepare and present sermons, I decided preaching wasn't for me. It was nerve-racking and unpleasant. I was shocked when the professor took me aside at the end of my second sermon and said, "You obviously have a real gift for this."

Oddly enough, I didn't enjoy preaching at first, in part because I didn't think I was very good at it. Later during an internship at a church, the pastor said, "Shane, it would be a real loss for the church if you didn't become a pastor; you are a natural at preaching." By the end of my seminary education I had been given the preaching award that year. All of this feedback came from the outside, not the inside. My self-assessment of my skills had not been aligned with the external assessments. Skills and talents are determined from the feedback we get from the outside, not the inside.

It matters whom you get feedback from. Some people will envy you, and their feedback may be a subtle effort to undermine you. Others may not be qualified to make an assessment. They may not understand what you offer and may misjudge it. Still others may be biased if they hope to flatter you, or if they simply love you and don't want to hurt your feelings. However, when you get feedback from a broad group of qualified and appropriate people over time, it can be a reliable and instructive mirror. Passion comes from the inside; talents are affirmed from the outside. Pay attention to the feedback from your environment to determine your skills.

> *Passion comes from the inside; talents are affirmed from the outside.*

Perhaps the most important point here is that I find people are capable of far more than they dream of. I believe there is almost no limit to the skills you can acquire if your passion is strong and your focus is right. While our desire is born on the inside, and skills are assessed from the outside, we must recognize that the desire is the fuel for skill development. Plug into the desire with clarity and focus, and the skills you can acquire will go beyond what you thought possible.

Plug into the desire with clarity and focus, and the skills you can acquire will go beyond what you thought possible.

Developing and exploring your aptitude is an important part of living your purpose. Everyone is good at something; you have to learn what it is. Some talents come naturally. A friend of mine is a mechanical engineer. He has specific training about how things fit and work together, but he also possesses innate talents in this area. Not long ago his company was building a new airport terminal. The ceiling was quite a challenge. The terminal was several football fields in size, and the design called for mostly hidden or inconspicuous load-bearing supports. A team of engineers had worked on it for some time but couldn't seem to find a way to make the architect's vision work. My friend, who was less experienced than the other engineers, was brought in to learn. After considering the problem, he went home that night and played with his son's Legos for a few hours. The next day he brought a Lego building in to show the team how they could solve the problem. They did computer renderings, complex math, and various tests to find out if his design would work. They ultimately implemented it. The next time you walk through the Denver Airport, remember that some part of the design was born of playing with Legos.

Eventually most of us will discover some limit to our skills. I played hockey and practiced it a lot. I wasn't too bad, I enjoyed it, and wanted to get better. So I went to summer hockey schools and worked out in the off season. I never grew much beyond average in my peer group. I maxed out. I didn't have the innate speed, the strength, or the killer instinct that many of my more accomplished peers had. However, when you reach a limit in a skill, it is often due to a waning in your desire. Never underestimate the power of your desire. If you are feeling stuck or lacking confidence in your competence, check in with your desire. It may be that you have lost touch with it, and when you reconnect to that power source, you will be spurred on. It may also be that your desire is evolving and it's time to listen to its call to reach for something new.

Then there are the skills we have never even tried to develop, the ones that lie dormant. These are the skills we get to discover along the way. Our desire or values may lead us to uncover skills we never knew we had. What if Michael Jordan spent his life as a golfer and never once picked up a basketball? Jordan is a pretty strong amateur

Our desire or values may lead us to uncover skills we never knew we had.

golfer. At the time of this writing, he was shooting in the midseventies. But he is nowhere near as good a golfer as he was a basketball player. He was one of the greatest basketball players the world has known. Sometimes it's just about trying different things and monitoring the feedback we get over time. This is certainly the case in our younger years.

The most common mistake I see is that people invert how to identify passion and skill. Passion is something that can be found only within, but people often borrow from the outside without knowing it. Skills are often determined by our self-assessment, which is rarely reliable because it's often either inflated or demoted. Determining a skill is best assessed by those on the outside who are qualified to assess them.

BRING WHAT YOU WANT INTO FOCUS

Once we have calibrated our desires (what we want), values (what matters to us), and skills (what we are good at), we are on our way to living the answer to the question *Why am I here?* If you have some initial clarity, it can be a helpful exercise to hone your desires in concrete ways. Here are a few rules of thumb when naming and defining what you want.

1. A well-formed desire should be framed in the positive rather than the negative. Because

energy follows attention, we tend to align our resources around that which we name, whether it's what we're after or not. The outcome of "I want more balance and rest" is generally more effective than the outcome of "I want to stop working so much."

2. A desire should be focused on that which we control. Many things in life, like the decisions and desires of others, we don't control. Living our directive may involve other people, but if it is mostly dependent on other people changing what they do, think, or feel, we will be disappointed.
3. Consider the internal and external resources you have available to you to achieve this desire. Are there any resources you will need to acquire (e.g., time, courage, schooling, money, etc.)? Are there any skills you need to develop?
4. What are the life consequences if you were to achieve this outcome? Every choice comes with a cost; that cost is ecological. In other words, every part of your life will likely be affected. It may also have an impact on the lives of others, society, or the world. Can you accept the ecological consequences of your choice? It is crucial to be clear on this before you commit to action.

5

WHAT IF I WANT SOMETHING OTHERS DON'T WANT ME TO WANT?

Our relationships have an extraordinary power to distort, prevent, or propel our sense of purpose. In this life, we don't get to pursue our purpose in isolation. A relationship has the potential to support or derail our best-laid plans. This applies to nearly any relationship, whether with our parents, spouse, children, employer, or friends. The question when it comes to relationships isn't merely about what we want or what they want; it is also a question of power and responsibility. The question is really two different questions:

First, what if I want something someone else doesn't, but I don't have the power to fulfill it? What if I want a promotion, but my boss won't promote me? What if I want to date or marry someone, but she doesn't want to be with me? What do I do with my desires when it appears someone else has the power to fulfill or withhold them?

The other related question is the opposite problem: *What if I want something someone else doesn't, and that person has no power over my decision?* What is my responsibility to them in that case? What if I want to end a relationship and my partner wants to continue? What if I want to let an employee go, but she needs the money and wants to stay employed? What if my parents want something for me that I don't want? What is my responsibility to another person when I have the power to shape his fate? What if following my purpose will have a negative effect on others?

These are important questions. To answer them, we have to step back and understand something about the way relationships help us become more of who we are. It begins by understanding how relationships serve as the primary mechanism in our own growth and expansion in this life. By getting clear on the innate processes that conspire to help us, the answers to the questions above become more apparent.

> *Relationships serve as the primary mechanism in our own growth and expansion in this life.*

When I was a child, my older brother and I used to wrestle. He was bigger and stronger, so it wasn't much of a challenge for him. Sometimes when he was bored with winning, we would engage in a game of strength and balance that was a bit more collaborative. Facing each other, we would clasp hands and back up as many steps as we could, in an attempt to hold an A-frame posture as deeply and as long as possible. The pressure increased with each step back and threatened to destabilize us both. The goal was to see how close to the ground we could get the apex of the A without falling. Often the temptation to turn the collaboration into a competition was too great. On a regular basis one of us would turn on the other. At a certain point, once each of us was wholly dependent on the other for balance, he might jerk back, pulling me forward. I would go crashing to the ground as he stepped forward, using my momentum to push himself back to his feet. Then we'd get up and do it again.

This childhood game is a metaphor for a phenomenon known in nearly all close relationships. It's what happens when our own emotional well-being depends upon what others think, feel, do, or say.

The A-frame posture shows us in physical terms how emotional dependency functions. Basically my emotional balance depends on another person, just as my physical balance depended on my brother. This is how nearly all relationships begin. We enter this arrangement by mutual agreement and expectation. The togetherness of the A-frame is meant to provide a sense of safety and security in a family, marriage, business, or any partnership. If both people are committed to the same goal and want the same things and trust between them is strong, this arrangement works beautifully.

However, eventually one person will want

something the other person doesn't, or will want it to a lesser degree. Then the A-frame arrangement mostly creates frustration, anxiety, and insecurity. And that's when the drama kicks in. As anxiety rises, what was once safe becomes threatening; what was once a comfort becomes stressful. Herein lies the problem with many relationships. What started as a safe harbor becomes unstable seas. This dynamic is born from A-frame emotional dependency.[3]

As anxiety rises, what was once safe becomes threatening; what was once a comfort becomes stressful.

The moment we come into the world, we are wholly dependent beings. We depend on our parents for everything. As we grow, we learn that when Mom or Dad are happy, we feel safe. We unconsciously learn the importance of making them happy. We later learn to apply this same orientation to others. We learn to depend on the opinions of friends or partners for our well-being. This can cause us to lose sight of what's important to us and what we are here to do in the world. Part of becoming an adult in this life is learning to stand on our own two feet and depend less on the opinions, expectations, and emotions of others. That doesn't mean we ignore the desires or emotions of others; it means that our sense of self is not bandied about by their experience of us. The first and most important relationship and responsibility is always to ourselves.

In general, an A-frame relationship is one of the most powerful forms of white noise that drowns out the One Voice from within. When our well-being is heavily dependent on what other people think, feel, say, or do, our sense of purpose is deeply shaped by one of three drives: (1) the need for approval from others, (2) the need to get away from others, or (3) the need to control others.

In general, an A-frame relationship is one of the most powerful forms of white noise that drowns out the One Voice from within.

THE THREE MOVEMENTS

When our well-being depends on the desires or decisions of others, we typically engage in a variety of strategies to manage the tension this causes. A great deal of energy is unconsciously devoted to dealing with differences. When dependence is high, we generally employ some version of one or more of these:

1. *We comply.* We may accommodate to the needs others so much that we absorb their desires as our own, forgetting ourselves in

the process. This way tends toward overfunctioning and overhelping, often taking responsibility for the emotional reactions and needs of others while unconsciously neglecting or ignoring our own. In this strategy we are less inclined to stand up for ourselves and tend to take on a martyr or victim mentality. The basic belief is, *If I can do enough to make the other person happy, maybe he will notice what I want and do the same for me. He will also like me more and not leave me.*

2. *We assert.* We may seek to control, manipulate, or intimidate in an effort to change what other people want. This way tends toward underfunctioning in a relationship. Here we fail to carry our own weight. Instead we make others responsible for our feelings. In this strategy we are less inclined to confront ourselves and take responsibility for the part we play in creating relationship difficulties. The basic belief is, *Other people are acting in ways that make me upset, frightened, or angry. My job is to figure out how to change who they are or what they want, so I can feel safe or happy.*
3. *We distance.* We may create distance or in some cases cut off all contact in a relationship in an effort to remove the conflict. If a

person finds the emotions of a relationship too intense, he may be unable to tolerate the anxiety and conflict that come when people want different things. In his effort to lower the emotional intensity, he looks for exits from the relationship or withdraws. In this strategy we tend to avoid others and ourselves and become out of reach. The basic belief is, *I don't feel safe in this situation; it's better to keep my distance and stay out of all the emotional drama whenever possible.*

These three relational movements can be simplified as a movement *toward* others, *against* others, or *away from* others.[4] We all have each capacity in us, and all three can be expressed in positive (high-functioning) or negative (low-functioning) ways.

> *These three relational movements can be simplified as a movement toward others, against others, or away from others.*

- The positive side of moving *toward* uses gestures of support, compassion, sacrifice, or love. It also includes honest, open acknowledgment or expression of needs.
- The positive side of moving *against* is about asserting boundaries and letting people see

our viewpoint even when they won't like it. It says, "This is the line where I end and you begin." It also includes protecting those who can't protect themselves.

- The positive expression of moving *away* is about creating space to gain enough objectivity or wisdom to observe and seek to understand. This movement includes a return to reengage a relationship with better clarity and less reactivity.

When dependency is strong in a relationship, or you find yourself in an unconscious and reactive mode, then typically the low-functioning, or negative, side of these movements arises. When expressed this way, these strategies increase the level of conflict.

The negative form of moving *against* forces the other person to give in. This usually accomplishes the appearance of subordination in another. It achieves peace through coercion or suppression, which is always temporary. The problems return, often with much greater intensity, but indirectly. An asymmetrical warfare ensues; the one who feels subordinated will learn hidden ways to sabotage when he feels bullied or controlled.

The negative expression of moving *toward* has a more intricate method of relating. One person pretends to imitate the desires of the other, removing the appearance of tension and conflict. This strategy appears magnanimous, gracious, and adaptable. However, when these desires are not aligned with the person's truth, over time it takes a toll. She may experience depression, repressed resentment, passive-aggressive behavior, hidden addictions, and other ways of acting out. This strategy most often leads to self-destructive behaviors.

The negative side of moving *away* means disengaging, cutting off, or even exiting from the relationship. The difference in desire vanishes because the relationship is gone. This may be a temporary strategy or a permanent one. Generally, this person has difficulty asserting her truth and needs, so she seeks to protect and preserve herself from a safe distance. Unless differences or anxiety are dealt with honestly, this strategy usually leads to a highly detached form of relating.

Everyone uses all three strategies at different times and in different relationships. While they all come as standard equipment in each of us, we tend to default to one of them more easily. We often learn these patterns by either imitating or reacting to a parent. Usually we find that our chosen pattern is either similar to a parent's approach, or in direct opposition to it.

Perhaps you can see which movement you tend

toward in life—toward, against, or away from. The universal tension that emerges between two people wanting different things in any relationship can be very discouraging. However, there is another way to understand the function of this tension. What if this is actually a built-in mechanism designed to inspire our growth and expansion in life? What if we face and engage this gridlock with a sense of hope and expectation? If we heed its call, many of our desires can become fulfilled in ways we never expected and couldn't have engineered. To do so, our focus of attention must shift away from the other person and toward our self.[5]

Our focus of attention must shift away from the other person and toward our self.

THE MARKS OF SELF-MASTERY

A-frame relationships are the result of a fundamental human struggle to manage two opposing forces: the drive to be connected to others in close relationship, and the need to maintain a separate sense of self. Much of human development, purpose, and potential depends on our ability to manage and integrate these seemingly opposing forces meaningfully. People who do this successfully show high levels of self-mastery and have a far easier time finding and living their purpose. A person aligned with the One Voice will demonstrate the marks of self-mastery, which include:

- Awareness.
- Courage.
- Kindness.

Awareness. Our eyes help us see everything in the world, but they cannot see themselves without a mirror. This little paradox also operates when it comes to knowing ourselves. It is easy to maintain an awareness of other people and their problems or failings. We may even unconsciously adopt the opinions of others we respect, without having checked in with our own. But self-awareness is different. True awareness of the self requires a willingness to look in a mirror and reflect on who you are. As you cultivate this kind of consciousness, it becomes a transformational tool—a bright light on the path.

It begins with the knowledge of your needs, your resources, your feelings, and your desires. Self-awareness also includes the ability to recognize your unhelpful emotional patterns and habits of thought that get in the way of what you want. These are the rocks in the road. Awareness involves tuning in to our feeling states and learning to remain grounded and nonjudging as we observe what is. This helps to keep us connected to our most reliable guidance system, which is our feeling state, while not becoming flooded or overwhelmed by our emotional reactions. We learn through self-awareness how to maintain a solid footing and self-composure. When we are connected and have knowledge of the self, we enter the world with a new clarity and direction.

Awareness involves tuning in to our feeling states and learning to remain grounded and nonjudging as we observe what is.

Much of my work as a coach involves the process of holding up a mirror to help people see who they are. Of the dozens of tools and techniques I've studied, one of my favorites is something called the *Enneagram*. This is a personal-development tool, rooted in ancient wisdom traditions, that identifies nine basic personality types and shows the unique patterns of thought, feeling, and behavior expressed by each type. However, it is far more than a static personality-typing system. It is very dynamic and has many layers of wisdom.[6] At the heart of the Enneagram is a mirror designed to help you see what you cannot see on your own. The system helps shine a light not only on our shadows, but also equally on the beautiful gift at the center of our being. When we wake up, we begin to see just how powerful we are in creating our own misery, barriers, and difficult relationships in life and work. We also see the unique path that helps us activate more resources and get more of what we want. When coaching people, I often fast-forward the practice of self-awareness by introducing them to their Enneagram type. It provides a shared language and a shortcut to many of the important conversations required for transformation.

Courage. Knowing who you are and what you want is one thing. But it is quite another to admit it to yourself and others. Emotional courage is the ability to *reveal* who you are rather than *present* who you are. Self-presentation involves high levels of self-monitoring designed to give an impression to which others will respond with approval, admiration, or acceptance. Self-revelation involves telling the truth, taking a stand, and showing vulnerability regardless of the reactions of others.

Emotional courage is the ability to reveal who you are rather than present who you are.

Emotional courage means you are willing to risk possible rejection and disapproval, perceived failure, or potential conflict in order to pursue the future you imagine. This may include setting clear boundaries for yourself or others. It takes courage to realize you are not responsible for other people's happiness, and they are not responsible for

> *Emotional courage burns away your fears and compels you toward what you want with confidence and clarity.*

yours. Emotional courage burns away your fears and compels you toward what you want with confidence and clarity, but without excessive attachment to the outcomes. This courage becomes a kind of fuel for the fire in your belly.

True courage is also the ability to have your feelings and not insist that others join you in them; otherwise, you're making an attempt at emotional control, manipulation, or bullying. It takes courage to be vulnerable in front of others and accept that others may not share your feelings.

Courage awakens in us when we get clear on our commitments. Our commitments are born from our deepest desires. But our desires turn into commitments when the desires become decisions or actions. A commitment is something for which we are willing to suffer. If courage is hard to come by in life, then it is worth asking, *What am I committed to? What am I willing to suffer for?* The answers to these questions are an important indicator of our commitments. Connecting to our commitments is the spark of emotional courage.

Kindness. To know who you are and to admit the truth about what you think and feel are critical to self-mastery. But they are incomplete without kindness or the ability to communicate your truths with a consideration of your impact on others. Truth telling is sometimes an excuse for cruelty. "Well, I was just being honest..." might be used as a cover to act punitively or speak judgmentally toward someone. However, kindness isn't just about being nice so other people will like you. It's born of a genuine appreciation of self and others.

Kindness involves the ability to see differences in other people without judgment or an insistence that they change who they are in order for you to feel OK. It is the capacity to take ownership and full responsibility for the life you create. Here you refuse to blame, avoid, or control others. The practice of kindness is also a way of nurturing flexibility of mind and method. This is how you remain open to the endless possibilities and pathways to achieve your goals.

This trait also involves extending kindness to yourself. To accept and appreciate yourself as you are (and to forgive yourself where necessary) is a critical capacity on the path of self-mastery. A loud driving voice in your head with critical messages may seem familiar and even motivating, but the inner critic is actually a shackle around the ankles of your potential. True inspiration and potential come

> *True inspiration and potential come from self-acceptance and nonjudging kindness.*

from self-acceptance and nonjudging kindness. My observation is that this aspect of self-mastery is the most difficult to develop and the most powerful once you experience it.

Cultivating self-kindness begins by understanding that you are in a relationship with yourself, whether you know it or not. How you view and treat yourself will be one of the definitive factors in your capacity to express kindness to others and develop self-mastery. To bring this about, take a moment and think of a best friend, a lover, or a spouse. Maybe these are the same person. Think about how you feel toward them. This is someone whom you regard with deep appreciation, for whom an easy love, respect, and admiration flows. When those feelings are active, how do you speak to this person? How would you convey your feelings to the person? What would you be willing to do for the person if he or she was struggling in some way and needed support, protection, or care?

However you answered the question above, now apply the same benevolence and words to yourself. Are you able to speak those same words to yourself and mean it? For some, this will not come easily, which may mean we've grown so accustomed to the inner critic that we depend on it to feel OK. Connecting truthfully with expressions of kindness, love, and appreciation directed at yourself can be difficult but catalytic in our transformation.

If this exercise felt forced or you couldn't think of anything, start smaller. Consider aspects of yourself that are easy to appreciate, especially those you don't have control over. What about your ability to breathe, think, feel, or love? It could be your eye color, which sounds ridiculous, but the point is to practice the muscle of appreciation toward yourself.

Whatever you focus on will begin to amplify. *Energy follows attention.* If you are fixated on your blocks, limits, and shortcomings, don't be surprised that they get stickier and bigger. When you focus your attention on your gifts, abilities, and strengths, don't be surprised when they deepen and expand.

The marks of self-mastery are traits we can cultivate, but they are also a practice we can perform in sequence. Self-awareness comes first; it can be difficult to admit and tell your truth if you don't know what it is. Kindness without some undergirding emotional honesty quickly becomes a method of approval seeking and may even devolve into manipulation and deception. True kindness to self is potent only when you are clear on your own commitments. The traits of *awareness*, *courage*, and *kindness* come not as stable achievements, but moments of maturity. This is not something we

> *The traits of awareness, courage, and kindness come not as stable achievements, but moments of maturity.*

finish one day, but continue to improve. The hope is that over time we will activate more of our abilities more often.

This is the endless evolution of the soul rather than a destination with a finish line or a diploma. Some of us are masters at one or two, but demonstrate deficiency in the others. Each of the three relational movements displayed in *against, toward*, and *away from* demonstrate different aspects of self-mastery, but deficiency in others. I have a history of pursuing *self-awareness. Kindness* to others has always been a value of mine. But *emotional courage* has been elusive many times in my life. Consider your life for a moment. Which of these three traits do you naturally excel at? Which aspects of each feel more or less natural to you?

- Are you clear on what you think and want? Are you able to share easily but also tend to be hard on yourself or others? This is an indication of emotional courage, and an invitation to practice kindness.
- Are you able to reflect on and think about who you are and how you may be different from others? Do you notice your particular patterns and habits of thought and how they get in the way in life, but have difficulty moving to action or telling your truth?

This is an indication of self-awareness, and an invitation to practice courage.

- Are you someone who is very kind and supportive of others, but neglects to assert your own needs and desires? This is an indication that kindness comes naturally to you, and an invitation to practice the courage to assert boundaries and tend to your needs.

Self-mastery is not for the faint of heart, nor is it always painful or heavy. It requires a willingness to look in the mirror with humor and commit to your growth. It means learning how to stand on your own two feet by taking maximum responsibility for your well-being, and at the same time allowing others to take responsibility for their emotional responses. It means managing the fear that comes with realizing you may impact, but can't control, how others feel or react to you.

To return to the visual metaphor, self-mastery represents a move from an A-frame to an H-frame relationship. The H-frame is a different kind of posture. Imagine two people, each carrying their own weight while shaking hands or remaining in contact. This physical image depicts what happens in the emotional process of those who are practicing self-mastery. In this posture, the strain between the two is lessened, the expectation is diminished, and the responsibility for your self is increased. Not only that, but the more independent and well-defined our sense of self, the more deeply we are able to connect with others. When we carry our weight, and let others carry theirs, we no longer fear others and their power in our life. We no longer have to risk trusting others; we are tasked only with trusting ourselves. Self-mastery allows us to be directed by our own inner guidance, one strong enough to relate in stress-free ways with others who may disagree with us.

The H-frame posture may at first appear as a kind of distancing when compared to the A-frame. However, we should not confuse differentiation with detachment. Differentiation is a well-defined sense of self, independent of others. Detachment is an emotional reaction driven by others. Distancing and isolation are attempts to get rid of anxiety rather than regulate it. The H-frame posture actually represents a stronger, more stable connection. This kind of definition and presence is also essential in situations where leadership is required.

We should not confuse differentiation with detachment.

When we operate in the H-frame posture, we experience greater freedom to choose our purpose and reach our potential in life. We learn to marshal our own resources rather than depend on others for validation. The amazing part about this process is we don't need another person's consent to act or grow. An H-frame approach to relating requires our own unilateral and independent action to work on our self, without needing permission or the participation of others. True differentiation frees others to make their own choices as we make ours knowing we have the internal resources to feel good in life.

If you are in an A-frame dependency in any kind of relationship, the move to an H-frame is almost never arrived at with mutual agreement. When you practice holding on to yourself and initiate this new posture, your partner in the A-frame will rarely appreciate it at first. In fact, he will often threaten you because he is now destabilized. He needs your side of the A to stand up.

You will have no power in whether another person chooses to grow or carry his or her own weight. However, if you can maintain a calm, grounded, and connected presence long enough, remaining clear in your intention without detaching in the face of their emotional storms, games, cutoffs, or threats, you can actually give them a chance to make a new choice. They are shown the doorway to their own path of growth. This is not the process of confronting someone else; it is actually the process of confronting yourself in front of that person.

Living by the directives of the One Voice means charting your own path based on your own internal guidance rather than on the feelings, thoughts, or behaviors of others. While this will be expressed with different kinds of actions, it is far more about the integrity of your own internal *emotional process* rather than learning new information, new language, or even new behavior. Your inner world is what must change for the true power to be unleashed. It cannot be faked or feigned. New emotional processes will inspire new language and often different behavior, but the process of differentiation and self-mastery means genuine transformation.

> *Living by the directives of the One Voice means charting your own path based on your own internal guidance rather than on the feelings, thoughts, or behaviors of others.*

A person living on the path of self-mastery appreciates who she is and who she is not, even when others can't. She understands that following her internal guidance in the face of resistance from others is not the same thing as narcissism. She is aware of this vice; however, her focus is on living with *self-awareness*, *emotional courage*, and *kindness* to herself and others. The differentiated person can see that the only way to serve the health of a relationship or even an entire system is to take responsibility for oneself first. Living aligned with the One Voice is a nonblaming, antivictim posture.

WHAT WE CAN CONTROL

With this understanding in mind, we return to the first question at the beginning of the chapter: What if I want something someone else doesn't, and that person has the power?

The summer between my sophomore and junior years in high school I worked as a wilderness camp instructor and counselor for sixth graders who were going on a weeklong canoe trip in Canada.

We had been warned about one of the kids in particular—Patrick. He came equipped with a suitcase full of meds to help manage acute ADHD and all manner of other lesser-known behavioral disorders. He was rebellious, often mean, disobedient, and, in wilderness settings, potentially dangerous. He was entertaining from a safe distance, but a menace up close.

Patrick was assigned to my canoe so I could manage the risk he posed. He and I would reside together for seven days in seventeen feet of aluminum surrounded by water and the wilderness. I was in the back to control the steering and keep an eye on him. He was in the front, serving as the primary engine. At one point, Patrick started getting mischievous. He began dipping his paddle in the water and letting it float back with the current, pretending to paddle. When I challenged him on it, he just stopped paddling altogether. I was exasperated and furious.

After attempts of verbal cajoling, there was no response. I tried threatening him in my best drill-sergeant voice. I employed scare tactics about impending storms and the risk of getting lost. I even thought about splashing him unless he started paddling.

All my efforts to get him to paddle were fruitless. I paddled harder, trying to make up for my recalcitrant camper. Towering charcoal storm clouds loomed in the west, and I knew this was trouble. We were still hours from the nearest campground.

It started to rain, thunder rolled in the distance, and I was getting angrier, wetter, and more anxious. I redoubled my efforts to get Patrick to paddle his load, but to no avail. He just sat there and ignored me. Having exhausted my repertoire of behavior modification techniques, I was resigned to forge ahead as the lone paddler. *How did he get all the power? Why did I feel like his hostage? I was the one in charge here.* After many hours, we caught up to the rest of the campers at the next campground well after dinner, around dusk. The storm passed to our north, and ultimately no harm was done. I remember replaying this in my head and wondering what else I could have done.

When I returned to the main camp, I shared my misadventure with the camp director. His response stays with me still and reflects one of the fundamental traits that come from self-mastery. He said, "Well, he's not an easy kid, but there is a simple way through it. Basically, you have to manage your own fear and get clear on your limits, then let him choose whatever he wants."

You have to manage your own fear.

I didn't understand. I wasn't afraid; I was angry. So I asked him to explain what it would look like to manage my fear.

He replied, "I would have said something like this: 'Patrick, here's the deal. I'll paddle as long as you paddle. When you stop paddling, I stop paddling.'"

It was simple and brilliant. But I still pushed back. "What if he never started paddling? Then we would have been stuck out there. A storm was coming and I didn't have a map. What if there had been a fork in the river? I couldn't afford to get lost." That's when I realized I was afraid after all.

"What you just said is the reason he had so much power over you. You took on all the responsibility for getting downriver safely, which meant he didn't have to take any. Instead, you should have created space for him to take some responsibility.

You have to manage your *fear* first. I would say something like, 'Patrick, if it rains, I've got a poncho that will keep me dry, and I've got food in the canoe for a few days, so I'm content to drift downriver. Eventually we'll reach our destination; it just may take a few extra days. You get to decide how long we'll be out here. I'm good either way.' I'm betting he would have started paddling immediately."

The wisdom of his strategy was instantly apparent. In a sense, it meant becoming more mature and developing some *emotional courage*. I had to accept that I couldn't control someone else's behavior. I needed to learn to manage my own fear and anger, respect him as a free person with choices, and let him make them on his own. Patrick likely would have experienced this approach as a manipulation, a threat, or an ultimatum. But in fact, all I would have been doing is managing myself in front of him.

The moment we got in the canoe, I entered an A-frame relationship with Patrick. I was dependent on him for my well-being and I neglected to take responsibility for my own fears. He knew I felt responsible for his well-being. So he had nothing to worry about, because he knew I would overfunction and pick up the slack.

The camp director taught me an important lesson that day about self-mastery and the importance of taking responsibility for my emotional reactions, managing my anxiety, and letting Patrick take responsibility for his. While it would not have been easy, it would have helped us both grow, and I still would have achieved my goal. I blamed him for our problems and couldn't see the way I had cocreated the issue.

There is a broader lesson from the canoe trip. It can apply to any situation where we want something other people may not want. Especially when we feel we don't have power. When we are in a place of relational gridlock, or feeling stuck on our path, it is always helpful to ask these control questions:[7]

1. What don't I control here?
2. What have I been trying to control?
3. What could I control that I haven't been?

The answers to these three questions in any situation can help triangulate the focus of responsibility and power. What you will find in the answers to these questions is a gentle guide that leads back to a familiar but also fresh answer each time. You will find your control is limited to you, specifically your thoughts and actions. You control where you focus your attention. You also control your words and behavior. These in turn will have an impact on the factors you don't control, which includes most

Your control is limited to you, specifically your thoughts and actions.

everything else. You don't even control your own emotions, not directly anyway. Your feelings are a bit like a rose. Nothing can be done directly to the rose to make it grow. Everything done to the rose aids growth indirectly. The soil must be tilled, the water must be right, the sun must be sufficient. Then the rose can grow. In the same way, where you focus your attention will have an impact on how your feelings manifest.

If I am focused on trying to control something I cannot, then I will begin to feel frustration and anxiety. If instead I focus on the factors in my situation I can control, I begin to feel more empowered, curious, and accepting. These new lighter feelings in turn open new pathways, possibilities, and solutions that are under my control.

This is the lesson from my mountain biking experience. You have a choice about where you focus your attention. Your point of attention will naturally draw more of what you are focusing on into your experience. You will naturally align with it even if you don't want it. If on the other hand you focus your attention more on what you want most and appreciate in your life, you will align with those things and draw more of them into life.

If you are in this situation, first reestablish your locus of control through the control questions. Next, turn your attention toward the desire behind the desire you are stuck on. A specific desire might be

"I really want to keep my job." Ask yourself why you want this specific job. What feeling does it give you? What is the larger and more basic desire behind the specific one you are focused on? The answer may be that it gives you the feeling of security, power, influence, and contribution, or the chance to play and practice your art. When you shift your focus away from a specific desire to a deeper, more general desire, it changes the way you see and what is possible.

Finding the more basic and larger desire beneath a specific one is a technique for increasing *adaptability*—the ability to create more avenues to get what you want. Remaining fixed on a specific desire whose outcome is out of your control will create frustration. However, if you learn to focus your attention on something larger and more general, or the feelings that undergird this specific desire, new avenues and options will naturally become available to you.

> *Finding the more basic and larger desire beneath a specific one is a technique for increasing* adaptability.

NOT EVERYONE WILL LIKE YOUR TRUTH

Now let's reverse our question. What if I want something others don't want me to want, but I have the power?

A number of years ago I found myself dissatisfied with my station in life. I no longer wanted to be in a particular role. But I had made choices and commitments that put me there. Over the years, a longing to chart a new course grew stronger, even as I tried to ignore it. However, I had considerable white noise, namely, my habit of seeking approval from others, which kept the One Voice at bay. People were depending on me to stay in my role. They would be angry and hurt and might even feel betrayed if I changed direction in life. I was torn between keeping a commitment I had made no matter what and looking honestly at the reality of my deepest desire. To follow my deepest desire would likely have meant the end of some relationships, as well as the irrevocable alteration of others. It would have meant people not liking me or respecting me in some cases.

The consequences of my decision would be significant and irreversible. I couldn't tell whether changing direction was an act of selfishness and escape, or self-development and emotional honesty. The internal and external static was substantial; it took some time and intentional work to clear away the white noise. Eventually, I accepted the truth: I wanted something other people might not want me to want. I understood that not keeping my commitments would rightly come with a cost. I also recognized I had made a commitment I wasn't ready to make when I did and breaking it would come with legitimate consequences I wouldn't like. Finally, I had to acknowledge my desire wasn't going to change and it was time to accept the consequences and follow it.

Yet for some reason, I continued to find myself stuck, unable to move forward with a decision to follow the path before me. I was no longer sleeping at night, my focus was lost, and I could feel the competing forces inside me. I was clear on my desire, but a desire and a decision are not the same. A desire is a feeling; a decision involves action. Without action, no movement happens.

A desire and a decision are not the same. A desire is a feeling; a decision involves action.

In an effort to get some help, I scheduled a visit with Judith, one of my trusted guides. While it is true no one else can tell us what the One Voice is saying, it is also true that a skilled guide or counselor can help clear away barriers to hearing it. Over the years, I had involved her in the most significant decisions in my life. By this point, the desire was clear, but I couldn't figure out why the commitment to act eluded me. During the meeting, I shared the places of confusion and the places of clarity. We talked about the consequences, the implications, how I got myself there, and the cost associated with my choices. After some time, she responded with a simple but profound observation.

"Shane, you seem concerned about not wanting to hurt other people. Is that true?"

I confirmed it was.

She went on to say, "You also believe that if you choose to follow your desire, you will hurt people, whereas if you decide not to do what you want most, you will prevent other people's pain, is that right?"

I reflected for a moment and agreed.

Then she hit me with a zinger. "Shane, do you realize your choice is not between hurting people and not hurting people? You don't get that choice now. Your choice is between hurting people with your truth and hurting them with your lies. These are your only options now. Which do you want? The choice is yours."

Her words took a wrecking ball to my self-defenses and self-deceptions. In that moment, I knew what I had to do. It didn't seem like much of a choice anymore.

I knew the truth of the One Voice. I had a responsibility to follow it so I could live with integrity. Naturally, I had many choices about how best to bring this about. But the basic decision was made regardless of how others would choose to respond. That was up to them, not me. I also realized that continuing to pretend I was someone else would cause more pain in the long run.

It occurred to me the reason I was staying in my current situation was not just that I didn't want to hurt or disappoint people, but that I wanted other people to like me and think well of me. My own desire was then hidden under the camouflage of my chameleonlike tendencies to be what others wanted me to be. Thus, it was a self-forgetting and even slightly deceptive form of "kindness." It was *kindness* without *courage*, which isn't true kindness—it's deception and manipulation.

My work with Judith served to deepen my *self-awareness*. Consider the metaphor of our physical height and weight. Height is something we can't change, a limit we must accept. Weight is something we can, through focus and commitment. Our inner shape has a similar quality: some parts we can change; others we cannot. But understanding which one is which is not as easy when it comes to the inner life. The process requires fearless release of outcomes. It means trusting that the wisest, most compassionate, and strongest part in us will stand up and not lead us astray. Some may use these words as an excuse to take off-ramps, but when that is the case, they loop back around and will find themselves confronting even more challenging costs. Life has a way of ensuring we learn what we are here to learn.

After a few years of engaging in my own process of discernment, I discovered I was fighting to change my height. I was trying to be something and someone I could not be. Very important people in my life wanted me to be taller than I was; some even depended on me to be that height. Yet when I finally named this problem and accepted it was not possible, all the struggles evaporated. I could accept who I was even if others couldn't.

The cost of my decision to change direction was significant. I lost money, important relationships, and a career. While the process was not without grief, ultimately I gained myself. During this episode in my life I learned a simple truth: sometimes when it seems like things are falling apart, they are actually falling together. As I continued to find my feet, I felt alive and more at home than ever. The internal shifts opened the way for a more fulfilling life that aligned even better with my deeper purpose.

Sometimes when it seems like things are falling apart, they are actually falling together.

This was a lesson in the subtle and overt forces others exert on our sense of purpose in life. Time and again we will return to the fundamental tensions between togetherness and autonomy, tensions that can resolve only on a deliberate path of self-mastery.

6

HOW DO I MOVE THROUGH LIMITS?

A woman who had been a physician in private practice for a number of years came to me one day for help with finding her purpose. After several conversations it became clear that she was a flute in the soup. While she was quite accomplished and well compensated for what she did, she was also restless and anxious in her profession. We went through a handful of the processes described in chapter 4 over several months. Eventually she uncovered a surprising and unmistakable desire.

To her great surprise, she learned that more than anything else she wanted to be a writer and a storyteller. This shift came with clarity but also no small amount of fear because there were several obstacles she would have to face. First, she had massive student loans and had invested a lifetime in school to get where she was. It would take some time for her to digest this fact. Second, while she was fluent in English, it was actually her second language. The transition to being a writer in English would involve a steep and uncertain learning curve of hard skill development. Third, she would need to get comfortable with a full reorganization of her financial life. Fourth, she would have to confront many serious internal doubts common to the writing path. Finally, she would need to prepare for the reality that many publishers and editors might never recognize her contribution or creativity. Anyone of these obstacles held the possibility of being a very real limit, one that could shut the door on a dream.

Sometime after our final session I followed up with her and learned she was well on her way to becoming a writer. She had made huge strides in the skills she needed through no small amount of energy and effort. It took over a year, but she had finally gotten an essay published in a magazine. Getting to that one yes required a number of noes. She had submitted dozens of articles and essays over a period of months and received countless rejections before getting a yes. It's true she felt demoralized at times, but remained undeterred thanks in part to the fire in her gut. Today she is working on the manuscript of her first book and has begun making an income through her writing. She has never felt more alive. The flute is now singing its song.

This story illustrates an inevitable aspect of living our purpose. We will face both real and false limits on the path. A real limit is a door that will not open no matter how hard we try, like trying to change our height. The reality of her finances meant she had to make sacrifices and adjust her lifestyle in very real ways if she was going to make it on her own. A false limit is a challenge that we can push through, like the task of losing weight. The series of rejection notices she received were not interpreted as a hard stop but as a natural and inevitable part of the process. She persisted through them all, and overcame these limits to achieve her goals.

Understanding whether we are dealing with a real or a false limit is crucial. Accept a false limit and we retreat from our quest prematurely. Push against a real limit and we fight a losing battle. The well-known serenity prayer best articulates the posture required for this work:

Accept a false limit and we retreat from our quest prematurely. Push against a real limit and we fight a losing battle.

> *Grant me the serenity to accept the things I cannot change, the courage to change the things I can, and the wisdom to know the difference.*

In chapter 3, we explored the reason discovering and getting clear on our desire is so important. The two techniques introduced there are relevant when it comes to dealing with limits. The first was to *focus on what you want, not what you don't.* When we focus our attention on our goals, our energy naturally tends to align around them. When we focus our attention on problems and barriers, we direct our energy and resources away from our goals. When desire is strong and positively focused, the challenges we face awaken creativity, activate patience, and fuel persistence. When our desire is focused and felt in us, nearly every barrier becomes a chance to create new solutions and awaken potentials. However, when the desire begins to wane or all but vanishes, even the smallest bump in the road becomes a barricade.

The second was to *maintain flexibility.* When I learned to relax my arms, my body and bike became more fluid and responsive to obstacles rather than reactive and combative. As a consequence, I was better able to make my way down the mountain with some ease and even harmony. Life will present no shortage of obstacles. Maintaining internal flexibility will often mean getting creative in how we experience our lives and keeping possibilities open.

To these two, I will add a third. The process for moving through false limits is rooted largely in our relationship to what we call "reality." More specifically, in learning just how much power we have to choose and create our reality.

CONSCIOUSLY CHOOSE YOUR "REALITY"

A friend of mine builds model airplanes as a hobby. He creates aircraft on a small scale with incredible attention to detail. He tells me all models are based on a principle called *selective compression*. In order to make a small version of a much larger object, you cannot include everything. You must select which details to include and which to leave out. Some details may need to be adjusted or clustered together. A miniature fire extinguisher may be included, whereas certain switches and dials on the cockpit dashboard will be left out or merged together. Knowing what is superfluous and what is not, while still giving the impression of realism, is the art of selective compression.

In life, we don't encounter an immovable thing called "reality." More accurately, we interpret reality through the five senses—sight, sound, smell, taste, and touch. Trillions of bits of data invade our senses every second. The five senses interpret and translate that data into what we call "reality." But the sensory receptors have a limited range. The range of hearing for the average person is somewhere between 60 Hz and 20,000 Hz. For

> *In life, we don't encounter an immovable thing called "reality." More accurately, we interpret reality through the five senses.*

the average dog, depending on the breed, it is somewhere between 65 Hz and 40,000 Hz, roughly double. As for the sense of smell, some dogs, depending on the breed, have a sense of smell approximately ten million times more sensitive than a human's. In other words, enormous bands of reality reside outside the interpretive range of our human senses.

In addition, the human brain has a finite processing power. It cannot possibly process all the information our senses are translating. This leaves a huge discrepancy between what we consciously experience and the rest of the near infinite stimuli we are immersed in. To help resolve the discrepancy, our brains employ a sophisticated form of *selective compression*. Reality is simply too vast and complex to fully experience, organize, or understand. So we learn to focus our attention on certain aspects of experience while ignoring others.

We automatically create an ever-changing scale model of reality. Our awareness of this simple fact is immensely helpful. The problem comes when we mistake the scale model for what it mimics, when we mistake the map for the territory. Selective compression consists of three basic techniques or strategies: *blocking*, *bending*, and *merging*. They serve a crucial purpose in helping us manage and organize reality.

Sunglasses help us see more clearly because they *block* certain frequencies of light in the same way our perceptual filters block vast quantities of information from being noticed and processed. We become highly selective about what we notice. Right now, as you read this, the bottom of your feet are interpreting and translating information and your ears are taking in incalculable stimuli. But chances are you didn't notice this until I directed your attention to it. I remember at one time I was in the middle of an office remodel. I had to make a decision about lighting options. For the next two weeks everywhere I went, every building and room I was in, all I could see was the kind of lighting that space used and how well it worked. As soon as I made my selection, I no longer noticed lighting fixtures. In short, we select our "reality" according to our needs, fears, hopes, or expectations.

> *We select our "reality" according to our needs, fears, hopes, or expectations.*

A man who is in love may notice that every song on the radio is a love song expressing some aspect of how he feels. Conversely, if he is going through the end of a relationship, he may notice that every song on the radio is about breaking up. In both cases he is likely selecting a reality that naturally fits with his focus of attention and expectation. Chances are the songs are about both things. In that sense both are real, but only one is experienced as "reality."

We also *bend* information in the same way that prescription lenses *bend* light to better focus it. In the case of our senses, we unconsciously bend what we take in according to our needs and beliefs. If I walk into a room and believe that no one likes me, I will likely interpret many of the subtle gestures people make toward me as confirmation of my belief, whether they feel that way or not. Over time, I may interact in a detached and aloof manner to protect myself from their rejection. They, in turn, may experience me as arrogant and, in fact, no longer like my company. In a very real way I have just bent or distorted the data and, in so doing, created a new reality that wasn't there before. In this way, I have become a creator of my "reality."

Lastly, we *merge* experiences and information in our environment by categorizing similar experiences as one and the same. These generalizations make it easier and faster to organize and attempt to understand our experience. For example, in the past you may have had an experience that shares similarities to the one you're in now. You might presume that because the experience is similar, the outcome will be as well. We call this "stereotyping" when it comes to our assessment of people groups. But this *merging* filter is active in nearly all areas of life. While it facilitates a more simplified experience, such merging sometimes limits other possible outcomes.

In point of fact, this generalizing tendency is an illusion; the life unfolding now has never happened before. In the same way you can never step in the same river twice, no two experiences are identical.

In short, we *block*, *bend*, and *merge* experiences to align with our expectations, hopes, or fears.[8] But reality is far more vast than we attend to. The way through limits is to cultivate an awareness of this fact to better awaken our adaptability. True flexibility is born when we become conscious of the ways we select and create our reality. One of our greatest resources in helping us get more of what we want is the ability to perceive a greater reality beyond the filtering strategies of the five senses. It means a willingness to challenge our assumptions about reality. More so, we begin to see the ways we are actually bringing about realities both positive and negative.

> *True flexibility is born when we become conscious of the ways we select and create our reality.*

The next time you arrive at a conclusion about your life that seems like an impasse or apparent limit, causing frustration or even despair, take a moment and examine the narrative you have created to describe your reality. Whatever narrative we tell ourselves, we must recognize it is always only a partial story, born of *selective compression*. That does not mean it isn't real; it means there is an endless array of realities we have simply ignored. This creates countless limits that are unnecessary and avoidable.

Testing our assumptions involves the examination of our lenses or selective compression strategies to see what possibilities we might not have considered.

Testing what we *block*:

- *Where is my attention focused? What details am I noticing?*
- *What other ways could this situation be viewed?*
- *What prevents me from focusing on other aspects or details? What might I be missing?*

Testing how we *bend*:

- *What story am I telling myself about this situation that may be a distortion?*
- *What assumptions do I hold about myself or others that may or may not be true?*
- *What fears, hopes, or needs do I carry in this situation?*

Testing how we *merge*:

- *How is what I'm going through similar to an experience from the past?*

- *What differences may exist that I haven't considered?*
- *What other positive possibilities and outcomes can I consider that I haven't?*

Your answers to these questions may surprise you. Each one probes in a different way, allowing our perceptual filters to adjust and open new doorways. Now is also the time to stay connected to your emotional guidance. When you change what you're focused on, does it feel generally worse or better? This is a powerful indication of which reality will best serve your goals. If it generally feels better when you think about your situation or life, you are on the right track. You will naturally go through some heavier feelings in the process, but if you are generally feeling worse as you progress, it's an indication your focus of attention is not serving you.

> *If it generally feels better when you think about your situation or life, you are on the right track.*

During my high school years, I took several algebra classes and did very poorly. I struggled with the concepts. It didn't take long for me to develop the following belief: "I am not good at math."

At the same time, after studying hard and establishing what I thought was mastery of the material,

I got a D on a multiple-choice biology test. Soon I added a belief: "I am not good at biology."

These limiting beliefs drove my perception of reality. They limited what I thought was possible. They left me feeling worse about my future prospects and myself. If it weren't for required classes in school, I would have assumed I was bad at math and biology and never made another attempt. The following year I was required to take a geometry class. The ease and enjoyment of the class startled me. The conceptual framework seemed intuitive and natural for me to follow. I did very well in that class.

After the abysmal score on my biology exam, my mom and I met with the teacher to see what could be done to improve my performance. My mom took one look at the exam and noticed the test questions and answers were all single-spaced. For years, she knew I had struggled with dyslexia, so on a hunch she began verbally asking me the questions I got wrong, in front of the teacher. She did not provide the multiple-choice options. To my great surprise (and the teacher's), I answered accurately all but two of the questions. This would have been an A. As it turns out, the problem was not my understanding of biology, but rather my ability to read the questions properly. I had developed a distorted narrative about myself and my abilities that was based on my initial experience.

The subsequent experiences dismantled my beliefs and challenged my *selective compression* about my abilities. I was able to update my beliefs and try new things without the same fear. Math was not a problem as a category; rather, one area of math seemed less intuitive to me than others. Biology was not an issue; instead, I had an access code challenge.

The examples above may seem like an insignificant kind of hairsplitting, but our subtle and unconscious assumptions about ourselves and the world will erect walls and preclude paths that remain completely open to us.

> *Our subtle and unconscious assumptions about ourselves and the world will erect walls and preclude paths that remain completely open to us.*

WORDS CREATE WORLDS

In addition to noticing our *selective compression* strategies, it helps to consider the power and limits of our language to shape the reality we choose to see. We use words to describe our reality and experience. Words are the basic building blocks of our beliefs and assumptions about reality. However, words by nature are incapable of expressing all of experience. Language is only an approximation. I can use words such as *sweet*, *tart*, and *tangy* to describe the taste of an orange. But these do not come close to the actual taste of an orange. When we describe reality in words, it is always a limited version, a thin approximation. Our beliefs, a product of language, limit us because they can't contain the totality of reality.

Our narratives or beliefs about life and others are a product of *selective compression* strategies and the limits of language. However, language has not only the power to limit, but also the power to liberate.

What I am describing here is not simply a magical view of words in which we can sculpt reality by saying the magic words. Nor is it only about keeping a positive mental attitude. The focus is on the deeper structures of the mind. Our habitually distorted assumptions and projections about the world or ourselves tend to create unnecessary limits in life. When examined and well framed, our beliefs can be a rich resource for overcoming barriers and creating new possibilities.

When examined and well framed, our beliefs can be a rich resource for overcoming barriers and creating new possibilities.

Awareness of these tendencies helps us see the part we play in the life we create. It helps us see the misguided assumptions and self-fulfilling prophecies, which may lead to bitterness, anger, and disappointment. This dynamic shows us that many of the injuries we experience at the hands of others are often perpetrated by us, against us. In this way, if we are victims at all, we are victims of our own devices. The more responsibility we take for our responses to others and the part we play in creating the struggle, the more empowered we are to choose differently. It becomes easier to forgive, extend kindness, and move on freely.

In simple terms, three basic techniques work together to help us move through our limits.

- Focus on what you want.
- Maintain flexibility.
- Consciously choose your reality.

THE THREE TECHNIQUES IN PRACTICE

Not long ago a company hired me as a coach to help with a crisis they were dealing with. One of the company leaders had made a series of high-risk personal decisions that began to impact the company negatively. The leadership of the company decided to suspend this person in order to figure out what to do about it.

The suspended leader did not understand the gravity of his behavior and was confused and furious with the way his partners were handling the situation. Each side began gearing up for a legal fight. The CEO told me they had removed executives in the past and had seen that things always got ugly. They were planning for worst-case legal scenarios and let their imaginations run wild with the calamity that could come their way.

They compared this situation to dealings they had with others in the past and noted the similarities. Each side engaged in a chess game of trying to anticipate the legal arguments and maneuvers the other side might take. Both sides dreaded what they assumed would inevitably become a long and costly process. Most of the people involved were experienced hands and had seen this kind of thing before. They knew how it would end—personal attacks, exaggerated claims of innocence and guilt, the tendency to dehumanize the opposition, defensive posturing, and vast amounts of money spent on attorneys' fees, settlements, or even a trial. In the end, they expected everyone would walk away bruised and bloody.

In short, all the strategies of *selective compression* were in place. Their assumptions about reality were unquestioned. If I were to suggest a different reality or the possibility of positive outcomes, it would appear to them as naive or a form of denial.

We tend to hold tightly to our carefully constructed narratives of reality. Attempting to undo them with an alternative narrative is not always easy or even wise. When I entered this scenario, the company leaders held a series of assumptions and beliefs about the crisis that were based on previous experience. They saw this as a very serious crisis that would end in a lose-lose situation. They used past experience as a generalization about the future. Their planning for the worst-case scenario served an important purpose: to inspire vigilance and manage expectations in order to prevent disappointment. However, it also served to blind them to other possibilities.

We tend to hold tightly to our carefully constructed narratives of reality.

The first step involved helping them question some of their assumptions. To illustrate that other outcomes were possible, I shared stories about similar situations I had experienced where the outcomes were positive. I acknowledged that their situation could end poorly, but there was a very real possibility that it could also end well. Planning for the best would also be necessary. As I talked about positive possibilities, one executive interrupted.

"I think you may be passing over just how serious this situation is. All due respect, I am not going to sit here distracted by unrealistic pipedreams when there's a real problem here. You can be in denial if you want, but not me."

This was an understandable response.

"I understand your point," I replied. "Given how serious the situation is, it's natural to be focused on the possible catastrophe ahead. And you are right; what I'm proposing is a form of denial. But denial is inevitable; our choice is not *whether* we will deny, but *what* we will deny. By focusing only on the negative, you deny positive possibilities. Either way, we are in denial; it's just a matter of which one feels better to you."

Denial is inevitable; our choice is not whether *we will deny, but* what *we will deny.*

He reflected for a moment and conceded. When I saw that he understood, I suggested we try an experiment to help him decide which kind of denial he preferred.

After a pause to consider, he humored me and granted the request. I simply asked to tell me what he wanted most, however unlikely. He thought for a few minutes and decided that the best-case scenario, though difficult to imagine, was that everyone would walk away feeling they had been treated with respect and that people would appreciate one another's efforts. When I asked him how it felt to imagine that outcome as a real possibility, he indicated it felt better than imagining all the bad stuff. I then asked the other executives to name their best-case scenarios. As they shared, it became clear they wanted the same things. This is the practice of focusing on the path, not the rock. It is also a way to shift what we are *blocking*. The rock and the road are real, but one is more helpful than the other.

As the days passed, we continued talking about the best outcome. They started noticing additional resources, approaches, and pathways that were previously hidden to them. A new flexibility of thought began to emerge. The process of aligning energy and maintaining flexibility can't be forced. Rather, it must be supported. As with a plant that naturally orients toward the sun, the key is placing it in the right environment and it will find the sun on its own.

When we first met, the leaders were using words like "crisis" and "triage" to describe the situation. This language has a great deal of power. It honors the intensity of emotion but also increases anxiety and stress in the system. Anxiety and stress are sand in the gears of any process. They block creativity and limit the number of options we can see. Using neutral or even positive language can help decrease anxiety. However, if the new

Anxiety and stress are sand in the gears of any process.

language whitewashes the situation, it will feel false and manipulative. The words we choose must reflect an important aspect of the emotional reality while still giving a more hopeful picture.

Instead of using the word *crisis*, I began talking about the *significant transition* the company was going through. I did not correct the language they used. To help the new language develop roots in their thinking, I described the transition as I saw it. My genuine belief was that the company was moving from a corporate culture that fostered unhelpful habits to a culture that promoted dignity, accountability, and integrity. We talked about the ways the executive in question was simply acting out some of what had been allowed in the corporate culture. While he was responsible for his choices, the other executives began to consider the part they had played in creating a culture that supported this behavior. They began to view this as an opportunity to wake up and grow into a new kind of company.

Growth is sometimes accompanied by pain. This kind of pain has an intention and a feeling of purpose. Their pain was leading them to a better place. We began linking the pain to their growth. By defining the situation as a natural form of growing pains, it no longer felt as much like a crisis, trauma, or failure. It was a normal part of the process of growing. People then had a choice not to see themselves as victims. This pain had purpose, and everyone had choices. Selecting alternative language allows us to consciously choose a different reality, one that offers more resources, options, and positive outcomes.

Another area that needed work related to the leader who had been suspended. The executives in charge described him as "a cancer in the company," "toxic," and a "liar" who was "unethical and immoral." Such language created an unintended consequence. The word *cancer* dehumanized the person and treated him as an enemy to be defeated. Language like this was working against the possibility of a positive outcome. Calling him a "liar" and "immoral" was a strong judgment that heightened feelings of betrayal and anger. While the emotions were understandable and real, they worked against the hoped-for resolution.

So we began using the language of "choices and consequences" instead. This leader had made a series of choices that made things more complex and had consequences at odds with the company's goals. I indicated that the leadership team now had several options. No choice is without consequence, but the question is, which consequence do you prefer? Neutral language helped put everyone on the same level; it gave maximum freedom to everyone involved and allowed a different dynamic of greater mutual respect to emerge. Each person was treated with full freedom to explore the options. The neutral language helped to defuse judgmental thoughts and emotional reactivity to one another.

As judgment subsided, people experienced more freedom to choose. A suspension of judgment is an important part of the process; change occurs more naturally in the context of free choice. When we remove judgment of self and others, we are free to make better choices in life from an inner compass. External motivations of rewards and sanctions are often short-lived. In general, the more space we make for the One Voice to be heard, the more we trust it for our choices and let the best in ourselves stand up and speak to the best in others. When this happens, wisdom, courage, and kindness align to support our preferred outcomes.

When we remove judgment of self and others, we are free to make better choices in life from an inner compass.

Over a period of months all the leaders involved moved beyond their conditioning to try to control the outcome. They could see that the choices they had made, which had gotten them into this crisis, would not help them out of it. A new path was needed, and they were ready to take it. Fortunately, they made many wise decisions. While there was some anger, fear, and sadness, no one let it get the best of them. They continued to trust the process, themselves, and one another. In the end, the outcome was far better than they originally expected.

Each person took responsibility for his part; the executive who had been suspended ultimately resigned from a place of acceptance. The leadership team expressed appreciation for his contribution to the company and found generous ways to support him in his transition out of the company. The company started to function at a much higher level of health, integrity, and impact. The leader who left was able to confront the consequences of his own choices and began making major changes for health and growth in his life.

Dealing with limits and challenges in life is inevitable, but there are habits that can help us overcome them. I noted three practices in this chapter: focus on what you want, maintain flexibility, and consciously choose your "reality." But they can be summarized as follows: learn to trust the One Voice, one that leads from a place of awareness, courage, and kindness.

7

ARE THERE ANY LIMITS I JUST NEED TO ACCEPT?

Daniel Kish is forty-five years old. An avid mountain biker, he can find his way in the wilderness alone, and he once lived by himself for two weeks in a cabin several miles from the nearest road. What makes these achievements so remarkable is one simple fact: Daniel Kish has not been able to see since he was a one-year-old. A rare and aggressive form of cancer attacked the retinas of his eyes when he was just a few months old. To save his life, his eyes were removed not long after his first birthday. Yet he developed skills that even sighted people might fear to try.

How does he do what he does? At a very young age his parents noticed he made strange clicking noises with his mouth. In time, they learned he was using these sounds to navigate his environment. He intuitively developed a skill that dolphins and bats use called echolocation. Each click bounces off objects around him and provides him with an acoustic snapshot of his terrain. In short, vision becomes music. He calls it "flash sonar." Daniel actually has the ability to tell you how far away from the curb a car is parked and whether you're driving an SUV or a sedan. He can tell if a pole is in front of him even when it is less than one inch thick. He can determine the density of an object whether it's a wall, a bush, or a street sign.[9]

Daniel's skills demonstrate the amazing way human beings can adapt, but also show an intriguing neurological feature of people. The human senses are ecological in nature. Although vision and hearing are very different senses processed in different parts of the brain, they draw from the same cognitive pool of resources for their functioning. Deprivation in one of the human senses will boost functioning in the others. The opposite is also true: stimulating all the senses dulls each one appreciably. This accounts for the near universal tendency to turn the radio down in the car when we are lost or looking for a street to turn onto. For Daniel, the total lack of activity in the visual cortex allows resources to be directed to the auditory cortex, hence his near supernatural ability to discern between the subtlest of sounds.

Daniel is also a fascinating case study in the power of limits. Facing closed doors in life may not be pleasant. Limits are rarely a welcome part of life, but they are incredibly important to our path of purpose and potential. Some limits we can't get beyond. These limits do more than stop us; they awaken capabilities and illuminate new paths. Limits work like riverbanks focusing and guiding the flow of water. The power of a river is derived in part from the banks. They work to provide both force and direction. Limits work the same way in life: they serve to direct and focus our energy. In doing so they give us clarity. When the path says, "This way is closed," we are spared the time and effort of fruitless searches. When the options we pine for disappear, the strain of too many choices lifts and we experience an unexpected freedom—a freedom from having to choose. The path is made clear. Limits play a major role in our development and our direction in life.

Limits do more than stop us; they awaken capabilities and illuminate new paths. Limits work like riverbanks focusing and guiding the flow of water.

Understanding what we are here to do arises from the creative conspiracy of our desire (what we want), our values (what matters to us, or what we believe), our resources (what we can do), and our limits (what we can't do). All four work together as guideposts along our way. The last one is often the most overlooked and misunderstood. True limits are sometimes about coming to terms with our identity, knowing and accepting who we are and who we are *not*. They remind us that cats don't bark, so don't waste time and energy trying to get them to. When it comes to living our purpose, accepting who we are not is as important as knowing who we are. It also means accepting a limit that we cannot control.

THE GIFT OF LIMITS

The nonphysical aspect of ourselves is as unique to us as our physical bodies. We come with certain traits, habits, capacities, and desires. Some aspects we have the ability to change. We can choose to grow and evolve many parts of ourselves in order to overcome almost any limit. Other parts are set for us, and no amount of effort will change them. When it comes to our inner life, the parts we can change and those we cannot are difficult to see.

The most unexpected and overlooked limit is our desire. The One Voice provides direction and desire, and in doing so it introduces limits. Wanting something implies that you don't want other things. This is a fundamental limit that should be honored. Others can try to persuade me, or I can pretend to want something else, but in the end this voice persists. Nothing and no one can change the true directive.

> *The One Voice provides direction and desire, and in doing so, it introduces limits.*

People can help give me language, focus, or strategy for what I want and how to bring it about, but the fire comes from within and has a life of its own. It presents both the engine and brakes in our life. Understanding and accepting the inherent resource and limit of our desire is crucial for living our purpose.

This was first made clear to me in my transition from working in advertising to becoming a pastor. In the year following my graduation from seminary I was still unclear about what was next. This was when I started working with Judith in earnest. Working with her and her practices helped me finally uncover and admit what I wanted most. For the first time I unearthed something that I knew came from inside me. It was nothing I had read in a book or borrowed from others. The clarity came in the language of desire. One day we did the self-inquiry technique (described on pages 77 and 78) together. As she gently inquired deeper, layer beneath layer of defense, self-judgment, imitation, and fear began to slough off. At one point in the practice I verbalized something very simple, so simple it hardly seemed all that original. It wasn't the words that were so important, but rather the way they felt in me. The words had weight, gravity, and presence. Somehow they felt both new to me and completely familiar at the same time. They encapsulated so much of the way I had lived my life up till that point, regardless of my career, but I had never put words to it.

The words that came out were, "I want to be a catalyst in people's movement." This may seem vague, but for me it was an anchor with a handle that grounded me. Obviously, my desire could be lived out in many ways. At the time my training, intellectual interests, and outside opportunities all pointed to becoming a pastor. The clarity I felt in this direction was acute and surprising. A strange thing happened when I made my discovery.

At first I was ambivalent. I even felt some unexpected sadness. As I considered the possibility of becoming a pastor, the job seemed overwhelming and unreasonable. I knew this wasn't a job, but a way of life. A pastor is always on call. The emotional energy and resources required for the community are the same as those required for your family. Both compete for a finite number of resources. Friendships are complicated by a different set of expectations and boundaries. Congregants project their feelings about past authority figures onto you, which causes them to see you as far worse or far better than you actually are. I knew if I listened too carefully I might believe the propaganda as well as the attacks. Ultimately it is an invitation to live in a glass house perched high atop a precarious pedestal.

You are given far more authority than you could ever hope to earn. I felt a powerful pull toward a way of life that seemed deeply challenging.

In this sense, the clarity I found caused me to confront limits, some pathways I would no longer take in life. Doors had now closed inside me, and I could no longer pursue those pathways with integrity.

Given how intense the experience of hearing the One Voice was, I knew there was no point in fighting it or questioning it. As a result, I initially resigned myself to this path. Of course, resignation and acceptance are not the same. They look similar in that they are both nonresistant. However, resignation is born of exhaustion or resentment, whereas acceptance is born of resolution and hope. Resignation is what happens when you give up. Acceptance is what happens when you move on. Resignation isn't always bad; sometimes that surrender is the first step toward full-blown acceptance. When we move on from a place of acceptance in life, we find gratitude, joy, and clarity on the other side.

Resignation is what happens when you give up. Acceptance is what happens when you move on.

The path from resignation to acceptance is important in the process of coming to terms with our limits. At the time I couldn't see what a gift my desire was. I was focused on the limits and losses that came from my guidance. And so I introduced resistance into my journey. The greater the resistance, the more our path will lead through grief or fear. This pivot in my calling was accompanied by grief until I was able to let go of what I felt I was losing.

Grief on this path is not a requirement for everyone. It tends to happen for those who are resistant and fixed on what they are losing. Part of my learning through the years has been releasing resistance and learning to welcome the gift of limits that my desire brings.

Our emotional life is our guidance system in living our purpose. Our feelings have an energy with a specific frequency of vibration, like strings on a piano. Feelings like hope, joy, and appreciation represent the higher frequencies; they show us when we are aligned with the One Voice, our true self, our deepest desire. Feelings like sadness, anger, and fear are lower frequencies; they show us when we are at odds with the One Voice or our truest self. The physical body is a perfectly tuned instrument designed to play the full range of emotions. Lower frequencies are as helpful in guidance as the higher ones. They should not be denied, disowned, or ignored, which is why emotional honesty is so important.

During this particular time in my life I held a stiff-arm aversion to what I had discovered to be my true self. My resistance yielded negative feelings of fear and sadness even though I found what I was looking for. As I learned to relax my resistance and embrace my desire, my guidance worked perfectly. In short order, hope, joy, and appreciation began to bloom in me.

The more immediately we attend to our emotional life and feeling states, regardless of what they are, the sooner we can consciously choose to correct our course and the sooner we remember the powerful role we play in creating the life we want.

> *The more immediately we attend to our emotional life and feeling states, regardless of what they are, the sooner we can consciously choose to correct our course.*

In the case of uncovering my purpose as a pastor, when I finally shifted my focus away from my fixation with limits, I was able to traverse the bridge from passive resignation to active acceptance. The career path I had chosen, along with all its downsides, was still there. But now the fear was gone. Fear is our conditioned, habitual response to danger. When it serves as a signal, it brings greater awareness and is quite useful. However, when fear is experienced as trauma or blocks our purpose, it can be debilitating.

When I finally started serving as a pastor, some of my fears were realized. However, because I had shifted my focus of attention, it changed the way I experienced these challenges. They were no longer threats to my happiness. They did not cause me to doubt my choice. In fact, the challenges hardly troubled me the way I feared they would.

The trials were simply part of who I was, not something outside me that I had to fight against or was a victim of. A friend once asked, "How do you handle such a difficult job?" My first thought was, *It's not exactly working in the coal mines.* Then I remembered I had had the same feeling he did at one time. I understood what he was asking, but the question no longer made sense. It felt a bit like being asked how I handle the challenge of being six feet tall. My height comes with advantages and limitations, yet I don't spend a whole lot of time fixed on all the problems it brings. It is just who I am.

The most immediate and significant limits are the ones on the inside. The more we focus our attention on the positive clarity of our desire, the less likely we will be distracted by the sense of loss or the fear of the unknown. Desire

> *The most immediate and significant limits are the ones on the inside.*

is a torch that keeps the distractions at bay. Keep it close at hand in the face of perceived limits.

> *Desire is a torch that keeps the distractions at bay. Keep it close at hand in the face of perceived limits.*

Living and listening to the One Voice is a subtle art that ultimately puts us more in touch with much larger reality. It allows us to accept and respond to real limits. That same voice also gives us the courage to move through false limits.

When we do this, we learn that the One Voice works like a river. As water flows, it has a way of accepting the limit of gravity without protest. It just flows to the lowest point. Along the way it will encounter banks, rocks, trees, and changes in the terrain. The water simply redirects in the face of these limits and challenges. While it always accepts gravity, the persistence and subtle power of the river eventually find a way around or through even the most formidable obstacles in its path. The One Voice, like that water, is patient, responsive, powerful, and free. When we let it live our life through us, obstacles and limits diminish, and living our potential is a natural consequence.

8

DO I HAVE JUST ONE CALLING, OR DOES IT CHANGE?

I'm just lucky, I guess. There's not a day that goes by when I'm not thankful for what I have," she said.

"Well, we're just grateful to have you with us," I replied.

My ninety-five-year-old grandmother and I were sitting at the kitchen table in conversation. I had just finished telling her how amazed I was that she was still so healthy and capable at her age.

She gazed out the window, then down at the crumpled napkin in her hand, and after a moment said, "I'm just not sure why I'm still here. All my friends are gone, and I'm not strong enough to do very much anymore. I don't feel like I can contribute much."

The words were spoken in a manner more curious than heavy, but they gave me pause. She is a reflective and kind woman who has lived long enough to know a few things about life. She grew up during the Great Depression, lived on a farm most of her life, lost her husband to illness twenty years before, and is one of the wisest women I've known. She has an easy quality about her that grounds me. The difficulties of life seem to roll off her effortlessly. On occasion she will say, "When bad things happen, you don't have to like it, but you do have to accept it." Simple words, of course, but when backed by hard-won wisdom they take on bold gravitas.

Here was this sage in her midnineties who had lived a life well and had done what she wanted most, which was to be a mother and a wife. Now in the dusk of life, with her husband and many friends gone, limited energy, and a family raised long ago, she was left to ponder her purpose once again.

Her comment reveals a simple truth about purpose. We don't answer the question *What am I here for?* only once. The question comes back at different times in life. We get clear for a time and then things change. New life conditions will bring about different limits and call out of us new capacities, values, and desires. The process of sorting out our path and living our potential cycles through different seasons and lasts a lifetime. The completion of each cycle puts a finer point on our purpose and points to deeper aspects, much like peeling back the layers of an onion.

> *We don't answer the question* What am I here for? *only once. The question comes back at different times in life.*

The implications of my grandmother's musing are far-reaching, but also quite simple. What we learn now about finding and living our purpose, we should learn well, for we will use these skills again. The process ends only when we breathe our last breath. If all goes well, on your ninety-fifth birthday you may be answering the question *What next?* The good news is, the more we practice these techniques, the more attuned we are to hearing the One Voice and the easier it is to respond and act.

What we learn now about finding and living our purpose, we should learn well, for we will use these skills again.

THE POWER OF TIMING

Our purpose is inextricably linked to our growth as individuals. As we expand and evolve inwardly, our external expression also expands. Our sense of purpose will naturally shift and change throughout life. The most amazing part is that each iteration depends on the previous one. Each new version builds on the one before, even when it doesn't appear so. That means wherever we are in life, we are exactly where we need to be. Trusting that you are in the right place at the right time can be both comforting and liberating, even when it feels like something is off or wrong or isn't working. Know that this is just the next step on the path, that more is coming, and that what you are going through now is building capacities and internal resources you will need for the next stage of your purpose.

My path appears, and certainly felt, like a series of very strange and unrelated turns—ad guy, seminary student, Mennonite pastor, author-speaker, megachurch pastor, executive coach—and who knows what's next. While I couldn't see it at the time, a thread ran through this evolution. Long before my professional career began in adulthood, a few of my friends in seventh grade gave me the nickname Freud. I guess it was the only word they knew to describe what I could do. I had an ability to help them understand blocks in their relationships and find other ways through them. I had a reputation as a guy you would talk to about your problems. This has continued through most of my life, and I have remained a perpetual student of psychology and human transformation.

Herein lies one of the strange features of our calling: our ever-changing purpose never changes. Within you is a constant drive, a deep purpose that really never changes. You came to express and explore and give something to the world. And that will evolve, expand, and shift. It's a bit like what happens physically. While I look nothing like I did as an infant, and every cell in my body has been replaced since that time, I remain

Herein lies one of the strange features of our calling: our ever-changing purpose never changes.

the same person with an unbroken continuity of existence.

Fortunately, this unpredictable and dynamic change baked into our purpose has a pattern built in. Learning the pattern can help us become attentive to transition points. In one sense, the cyclical patterns of calling mirror the seasons in nature: the beginnings of spring, growth of summer, harvest of fall, and endings in winter. Each new season of growth comes with different resources and limits. This is all about timing, an overlooked and underrated aspect of our calling. Our attendance to timing is crucial to this work. If we just pay attention, let go, and wait for a moment of inspiration to act, the timing will always be perfect.

Fortunately, this unpredictable and dynamic change baked into our purpose has a pattern built in.

Like the seasons in nature, we do not control the timing of purpose; these seasons have their own timing. Our only options are either to join these forces or to resist them. In nature, seasons are easily noticed and identified, but the seasons of life purpose are often more difficult to detect. They exist both in our interior states of being and in forces outside of us. We must pay close attention to perceive their changes.

When we recognize and participate with a

particular season, we find a supportive companion on our way. The process is actually quite enjoyable and filled with anticipation. We learn to conserve, focus, and deploy our energy and resources for just the right moment. When we take advantage of the natural timing of purpose, the impact and effectiveness of our energies are amplified. If I find myself out of sync with the seasons, the opposite is true. If I try to plant seeds in winter, the frozen earth will rebuff my efforts. If I seek to harvest in the spring, the fruit will be bitter. If I practice stillness and preservation during the autumn, when everything is crying out to be collected, I will miss the bounty.

When we take advantage of the natural timing of purpose, the impact and effectiveness of our energies are amplified.

Timing is a major aspect of maximizing our potential and purpose. The One Voice will prompt and inspire at just the right moment if we are listening to ourselves attentively.

WAIT FOR IT...

In chapter 1 I spoke about my experience of leaving advertising and attending seminary. Driving west across the country with my belongings in tow was an exhilarating experience. I left my life in advertising behind and imagined a new world of exciting possibilities in California and beyond. Seminary would be my way station as I sorted my priorities and plotted a course for the next step in my career. The prospect of wide-open possibilities was initially exciting. However, the multiplicity of options along with my lack of clarity about which way to go reversed on me. The stark reality of an unknown future caused more fear than excitement. As a welcome distraction, I buried myself in studies, hoping the fear would resolve itself on its own.

After the second year, I took inventory and noticed I had made little to no progress. Any inkling of what might be next eluded me. I had one year left to figure out what was next. The unknown loomed over me. Rationally, I knew this should be more than enough time, but I was itching for an answer or any indication of what to do next and found myself frustrated and confused. I went looking for interventions and help in the form of mentors, internships, and career counselors. Each effort offered new learning, but none of them could give me an answer. This was the winter of calling.

Winter is a season of stillness, preservation, and the unknown. In the north, trees both living and dead look identical. We must wait for spring to know where the life is. The only appropriate posture in winter is that of waiting and preparing, which requires patience, anticipation, and trust. In the realm of purpose, this can be the most challenging season of all. However, when we learn to recognize the season is upon us, something else is possible. Winter actually presents unique wisdom and resources. The gift of winter is that of a cocoon; it causes us to turn inward and provides the context and container for a unique form of transformation. During times of the unknown, profound changes are possible. We are invited to conserve our resources to prepare the way for spring, when new life requires a burst of focused energy and clarity.

The gift of winter is that of a cocoon; it causes us to turn inward and provides the context and container for a unique form of transformation.

Patience is a great ally during the in-between time of winter. This is a time of open-ended listening and inward attention, a time of exploring and unearthing desires. The One Voice may seem muted under the frozen earth, but it still speaks. The techniques outlined in chapter 4 (pages 72–81) for finding what you want are most helpful during winter.

By my third year in seminary I had been introduced to the practices above in my meetings with my friend and guide, Judith. As I began working with them, I sensed a simple and unmistakable desire within. Over time and with practice, a new clarity emerged. When I finally named this desire, it felt utterly new and yet completely familiar.

INTO ACTION

The day I experienced and articulated this clear desire was liberating. I felt like I had finally been given a rudder and a sail after years of drifting in a raft. I still had to choose which way to go, but I finally had agency and clarity. The shackles of the unknown had been undone, and now I could move. After some time searching and interviewing, a church in Phoenix, Arizona, which best aligned with my values and desire, invited me to be their pastor.

On entering seminary, I had told myself I would never become a pastor. But now after wandering in the wilderness, the path was clearly the most natural fit for the directive of the One Voice. I trusted my hunch and pursued it; all of my initial strident objections no longer held much weight. My energy was devoted to how much I needed to learn about this role and work. I wondered whether I had what it would take to be successful. Doubts about my skills in a new field were common, but I never second-guessed the decision. Spring is the season when desire transforms into decision. Spring is a time for actions, not waiting or testing.

Spring is not all singing birds and rainbows. The thaw is muddy and messy and the earth still cold and wet. The conditions of rebirth are not always beautiful, but they are hopeful. The pale-green buds have yet to tell us what flower or fruit will result, but we know something is alive. Winter, though harsh and barren, allows for wide-open possibilities. Spring breaks through with a clarity that narrows the options. Some pathways and possibilities came to an end inside me. I knew which trees were living and which were not and would need to be cut down.

Spring breaks through with a clarity that narrows the options.

In this season, new questions emerge and we may wonder whether we will master the new skills we need. It is a time of testing and acting on hunches and intuitions with no attachment to outcomes to see what fruit or flower will ultimately come. Spring is the time to live at our edge and see what might be possible.

GAINING MOMENTUM

The years following my move to Arizona were filled with extraordinary challenges and exciting experiences. However, the question *What am I here for?* was gone; the answer seemed self-evident. My energy and attention were focused entirely on the demands of raising a young family and the adventure of leading a rapidly growing faith community. I had much to learn but felt a deepening competence and confidence in the role. Internally I felt joy, connection, and gratitude even when things were painful or difficult. These experiences merely signaled another chance to learn and overcome.

During this time, the external feedback I received was also positive. The community I served was growing and reported greater levels of engagement. My first book, *The Hidden Power of Electronic Culture*, launched to positive reviews and higher-than-expected sales. Invitations for speaking and consulting came in from around the country. I was at the intersection of living my passion and contributing in the world. A seed had been planted in receptive soil; the tree was now established and growing. Following a harsh winter and a tenuous spring, the stabilization and growth of summer were deeply gratifying.

The questions of purpose mostly vanish in the summer. Instead, our energy is devoted to making the most of our impact and chosen area of contribution. Summer is a time of deepening roots and enjoying the expansion in our lives. While this is often a season of impact, recognition,

> *Summer is a time of deepening roots and enjoying the expansion in our lives.*

or wealth generation, it may not always show on the outside. Mostly we experience life as a well-tuned instrument in the hands of a skilled musician. We play the song we were born to play.

The transition from spring to summer is the move from a decision to momentum. During this season, the appropriate response is that of enjoyment and gratitude. The labor is often quite hard, but always coupled with a strong sense of meaning. In this time, most hardships feel like challenges that animate us rather than barriers that deflate. The One Voice speaks with clarity, we understand and accept limits more easily, and challenges are welcome as a great sharpener of skills.

EVERY BEGINNING HAS AN ENDING

Five years into my new calling, I began to experience influence I never imagined I would have. The church continued to grow and make an impact in the world. My second book, *Flickering Pixels*, outsold the first book, won awards, and led to a series of speaking invitations that put me in front of large and influential audiences. Mars Hill, a megachurch in Michigan with 6,000 members and 25,000 to 30,000 podcast subscribers around the world, invited me to become the preaching pastor alongside their founding pastor, Rob Bell, who was a longtime friend of mine. This expansion of success, impact, or influence are often hallmarks of autumn.

Fall is the time of harvest and abundance, when the fields are ripe and ready to go. Underneath all this, another more significant process is also under way. As the season wears on, we learn fall is also about decay, shedding, and preparation. During this time we take stock, learn to give back, and appreciate all that has happened. But the gift of abundance can sometimes mask the reality that everything with a beginning has an end. Fall initiates the decline and end of a cycle. Winter is on its way again. During fall we may be quite successful but we may experience an uneasiness or perhaps even boredom or disinterest in our achievements or role. Energy may still be there, but the fire and fortitude to push through external barriers may start to wane. Curiosity about other areas of life may grow.

During fall we may be quite successful but we may experience an uneasiness.

Five years after accepting my first pastorate, I made a decision to leave the smaller church and began serving at Mars Hill. From the outside this looked like a sign of having "made it," an unmistakable rise to greater influence among my subculture. However, despite appearances, I was also aware somehow that it was the beginning of an end. I didn't know what would come to an end or when, but I had a vague awareness that fall was upon me.

During this time I put forth great effort into my writing, speaking, and leadership. However, I noticed my enjoyment was not what it used to be. The once responsive and receptive soil was no longer so warm and welcoming. A year before, I felt completely at ease as a preacher, but now, even though the community was highly responsive, my sense of connection and excitement was waning. My lack of passion seemed to seep into any new projects and activities I attempted. Some of them had impact; others landed with a thud. My third book, *Selling Water by the River*, the one I was proudest of, launched. Despite my considerably higher profile and more muscle from my publisher, it never found an audience and seemed to have fallen through the cracks. What few reviews I did receive were very positive, but no one seemed to know about it. More important than the response from others, when I did hit on all cylinders, my enjoyment was muted and flat. The natural rising tide I had enjoyed in late summer and early autumn was now receding again. I knew this feeling, and realized I had a choice. I could swim against it, or I could join it and prepare for the natural cycle of an ending. I could accept it not as a loss, but as an invitation to another transformation. I began listening for and paying attention to how my interests were shifting, where my curiosities were focused now.

I had encountered barriers and unresponsive soil in life before. There were considerable external challenges beyond my control, but far more powerful were the forces on the inside. Ultimately, that fire in my belly grew dim, my willingness to suffer for my art and impact faded. When we are no longer willing to suffer for something, it is an indicator that our commitments are changing. The season of winter may be near.

> *When we are no longer willing to suffer for something, it is an indicator that our commitments are changing.*

During this time, my attention was taken up by a side endeavor that occupied only a small part of my time. A few senior corporate executives who had been listening to my sermons online approached me for coaching and consulting in their companies. I decided to give it a try and noticed how refreshing I found the pragmatism of corporate America. People in the companies I worked with didn't worry about dogma or ideology; they were interested in what worked to help unlock them in their performance. My approach to helping people get unlocked was getting results in ways that surprised and stimulated me. The work was immensely exciting; I was now passionately immersed in expanding my knowledge of the psychology of human potential through trainings, workshops, and readings. All of this was a clue. I could feel the risk of leaving the church. I knew some people would be affected negatively if I left. I also really loved the people I was serving. More important, I knew the cost of not following the directives of my desire. The One Voice was issuing its wisdom once again.

After much soul-searching and preparation, I chose to resign from the church and focus on building an emerging corporate-consulting and executive-coaching practice. I agreed to stay on while they found a replacement. I was quite surprised to have hit this internal limit at the top of my game. But I felt I couldn't stay in a place when my heart wasn't in it and still keep my integrity. It was clear to me—the time to conserve my energy and prepare for change was upon me.

I had been through something similar when I knew it was time to leave advertising. This time, I recognized the pattern. And this time, I no longer feared the winter. I knew the wisdom it has to offer and the possible transformation that was ahead. I was able to participate with it rather than resist or fear it. As a consequence, it was much easier to weather, even enjoy. The unknown became an ally in transformation rather than a bitter night to endure. I followed my new curiosities, knowing they were leading me. Don't misunderstand me—there were cold nights and stark realities. A sense of loss was felt on a number of occasions, but they seemed to be teeming with potential and meaning. This is the season of hiddenness and reinvention. A protective cocoon limits our impact and contribution, but it also provides the space for substantial change to occur. These are the seasons of purpose. Learn them well, for you will pass through them more than once in a lifetime.

READY, FIRE, AIM!

A sense of urgency often accompanies the process of finding our purpose and living our calling. It's a powerful aid that can fuel us to keep moving and searching. This same urgency can blind us to the incredibly supportive and resourceful gift of timing or seasons. For some of us the gap between impulse and action, or desire and decision, is very short. We are more likely to say, "Ready, fire, aim!" and see where the chips fall. Sometimes this leads to unintended consequences, missed opportunities, and regrets.

There are two ways to get a plane on the ground—you can crash it or land it. If you push an aircraft nose straight down, the plane will be on the ground faster but the damage will be extensive. On the other hand, if you land a plane in a gradual, controlled descent, attentive to timing, it may take a little longer, but the plane will meet the ground in just the right way at just the right time. Sometimes the best way to speed things up is actually to slow them down.

Sometimes the best way to speed things up is actually to slow them down.

A pilot will tell you a good landing involves a sequence of steps—choose your approach, check fuel flow, adjust to the proper glide slope, deploy landing gear, trim flaps, and so on. Each one of these is reversible or adjustable as you plan the approach. As we pay attention to timing, and notice the urgency, it's also helpful to ask what season we're in. If we are clear on what we want most, but something keeps getting in the way, or the world doesn't seem to be cooperating, or the consequence and the cost seem too great, then we know the fruit isn't ripe yet; if you pick it now, it will taste sour.

One way to manage the discrepancy between urgency and obstacles is to create a series of smaller steps toward your desired future, without making a major decision. Are there any smaller steps you could take to test the water? They should be reversible or adjustable so as to maximize flexibility and minimize the cost of a major decision. Each step can be experimental rather than final. Each step serves as the landing procedure for the plane. Each decision can still be adjusted or undone, the closer you get to the ground. A landing can even be aborted at the last minute if need be.

For the big decisions in life, especially the ones that affect other people or have irreversible consequences, it helps to widen the gap between desire and decision, between impulse and action. In the time between these two, we take inventory and ask whether we can accept the ecological consequences of our choices. A few moments of conscious thought will avoid years of frustration, pain, or confusion. For some people, pressing pause comes naturally; for others it may feel glacial. But the dividends are substantial. When we have the wisdom to wait for the right season, the fruit is always sweeter.

READY, AIM...AIM...AIM...

For others, the lesson may be the opposite. You may be a master at contemplating an approach, but in need of the courage to act; otherwise, you will overshoot the runway. The seasons may call for a time of evaluation, waiting, or watching. Pay attention to the wisdom of those seasons. However, a time will come when you will know which way to go. In that moment, there is no substitute for action. Action has a way of burning away our doubts, quelling our ambivalence, and plunging us into a thrilling adventure of the heart.

In this case, no virtue is more potent than courage, pure and simple. At times, I feel it coursing through my veins. I'm charged with the strength and motivation to push through limits, make difficult decisions, and speak my truth. Other times, it feels like a scarce and elusive gem hidden deep in the earth and out of reach. On those days, I want to crawl under the covers and go back to sleep.

> *No virtue is more potent than courage, pure and simple.*

However, the resource is not as elusive as it may first appear. Courage to act is not something that exists outside us. In fact, we already have all the courage we need, whether we know it or not. It resides within each of us in limitless supply. We are not tasked with creating courage, but activating it. The process begins by placing our attention on it.

If you are wondering where it is, then a simple practice can point you in the right direction. Think back to a time in life when you faced a challenge, a problem, or a barrier you were able to overcome. At some point, you needed courage to move through it. It could be a big decision you were afraid to make, perhaps leaving a job, entering a relationship, or making a high-risk investment. Or it could be something much smaller. Choose a moment you felt successful in overcoming a challenge. Go back to that moment and think about how it felt. What did it feel like in your body? Where did you feel it? What was the intensity? Assume the physical posture that courage gives you. Literally act out the stance. How would you stand? Where would your feet be? What would your legs, chest, chin, and eyes do? Focus on the moment you overcame the challenge. Where is the energy in you physically? What did the courage feel like in your body then?

Remember that feeling as if it were happening right now. Bring it into this moment. If you can feel even a small amount of courage from the past, you are feeling it in the present. This is not just a distant memory, but also current reality. You already have the resource you are searching for. Now turn to consider any block or barrier, any major decision, you face. Have this problem clearly in your mind and bring the physical feeling of courage into your body as a gift you give yourself.

> *You already have the resource you are searching for.*

After reading this section, you can try the exercise: Put the book down, close your eyes, and really feel the energy of courage in your body. Notice where it lives and how it feels. Focus your attention on it, and attend to it the way you might a newborn baby. You may feel it has movement, shape, color, or even a size. Whatever you feel, focus on it. Now, in this new state, the feeling of courage present, ask the question *What next course of action might be required to get where I want to go?* You may be surprised by the answer.

9

IF I FOLLOW MY PURPOSE, WILL I BE SUCCESSFUL?

When I arrived, I saw Tom already seated at the table. He seemed peaceful and relaxed. It had been a little over a year since I had last seen him. At that time, his life and everything in it had broken loose like an avalanche and nearly buried him alive. I was in his city on business and reached out to arrange a lunch and see how he was doing.

Tom was a charismatic and successful businessman with a tremendous amount of creative energy. He was always coming up with new ideas and had an ability to attract people to himself effortlessly. Recruiting people to his cause came with ease, and motivating them was never a problem. His business was both innovative and profitable. Others considered him very generous. Money flowed naturally into his life, as did friends and exciting new experiences. His wife and three small children rounded out the model of a successful man. By every metric he cared about, he was winning. Most important, he loved his work and was really good at it. Tom was living with a great sense of purpose. The confluence of his passion, values, and talents collided in a perfect storm of bliss.

What was less apparent was a long-standing propensity to distort and exaggerate claims. A natural-born salesman, he operated with a flexible definition of the truth. When it suited him, he could easily distort reality, misrepresent facts, or flat-out lie. His first lie was always to himself, and he often didn't even notice he was doing it. A strong sense of denial was more often the cause than malice. Once Tom bought his own propaganda, he could no longer see the lie, which made it all the more believable to others.

For years, this was his mode of operating. He was rewarded for it time and again, but eventually it caught up with him. Through a series of revelations, his world began collapsing around him as he faced serious legal trouble with his company and the possible end of his marriage. I met him just as his life began to unravel, and I became a coach through this season of crisis in his life.

Tom had a particular talent for avoiding the costs, consequences, and lessons of his behaviors. It started with his parents, who shielded him from most of the consequences of his mistakes early on. While this may have been misplaced love on their part, it fostered a belief that consequences didn't apply to him. He had faced failures throughout his life but always managed to spin the story, find a loophole, call a powerful friend, or use a technicality to stay out of trouble. The more we talked, the more I could see how rapidly and ingeniously his mind could create new excuses and ways of avoiding the costs of his behaviors. It was a remarkable talent that demonstrated how adaptable he had become. At the same time, he slowly began to confront the fact that he was not the man he had pretended to be.

At this stage in his life—he was in his early forties—the cost of truly coming clean was considerable. He could lose his job, millions of dollars, and his family. Nonetheless, he decided he was finished with taking exit ramps. Instead he chose the path of honesty and entered the painful but liberating process of learning some key lessons.

Tom began to face the truth he had long buried in his life. He confronted the elaborate web of lies he had woven and dismantled it before everyone's eyes, at significant personal cost. He did lose many of the things he feared to lose. The board fired him, his wife left him, friends turned their backs on him, and he lost a lot of money.

As we talked at lunch that day, I was inspired by his emotional courage and willingness to make such difficult choices for the sake of confronting the truth about himself. At one point he said, "I wish I had learned these lessons earlier. I could have saved myself and others a lot of pain. This has been the hardest experience of my life. My life isn't where I thought it would be, and I have so many regrets."

He paused for a moment and stared into the middle distance, digesting the gravity of what he had been through. I could feel his grief as if it were my own.

Then he continued. "But you know what? I finally have my integrity back. I feel healthier than I've ever been, which is worth more than anything I had before. When I feel sad about what I've lost, I remind myself that in so many ways it was never mine, because I wasn't me. It was all built on an elaborate collection of lies. It was the hardest thing I've ever been through, but I'm more me than I've ever been."

That statement hung in the air. It was a deep wisdom. Through his experience and because of his choices Tom had developed self-awareness and tapped into his inner resource of courage.

By all external measures, this experience would be considered a series of failures for Tom. He lost almost everything he had used to define his identity and sense of self-worth. However, after he made it to the other side, Tom had a different perspective. He was able to recognize that this series of losses brought about one of his greatest triumphs in life. He restored his alignment with his true self—a great success by his own reckoning. Prior to this experience, he never would have defined success this way. Today he is with a new company, in a role that suits his considerable gifts. He loves what he's doing again. The biggest difference is that now his inner life is aligned with his outer life.

The answer to the question *If I follow my purpose, will I be successful?* depends on how we define success. By external measures, you may find success elusive and unstable. Living our purpose and walking our path will not always mean more external power, money, love, freedom, or influence. However, if we consider a broader definition of success, one that includes the interior dimensions of our being, then success is far more likely.

Living our purpose and walking our path will not always mean more external power, money, love, freedom, or influence.

We must learn to define success differently. Our greatest success may occur when our path forces us to confront the shadow or negative aspects of our character or personality that no longer serve us. Success includes learning to drop our false self—the part of us constructed from our ego or in response to the wishes of others. The false self can be a persistent and sticky part of us. It was constructed for a reason, and may even have served us well for a season, but elements of the false self are training wheels for life designed to help us establish our safety and security. Eventually they must come off if we are to become who we truly are. Those who resist the natural process of growth will experience life and its many challenges as quite painful and even cruel. If we remain attached to things destined to disappear, we face an uphill road. However, life and everything it brings to us is there for our benefit. A hidden gift resides inside each moment, there to teach us. If we are awake to this gift, we may learn to become our true selves.

LIFE IS A SCHOOL

Life on earth is a school and it's not an easy one. We are here to learn and grow. The curriculum will involve challenges, losses, and limits. These can come in the form of job loss, the end of a relationship, seeing your dark side, illness, or even the challenges that come from material abundance and sudden success. In the face of any challenges, we are often presented with a choice. We can either face it head-on and deal with it, or take an exit ramp. This option lets us avoid a critical lesson if we want.

Life on earth is a school and it's not an easy one. We are here to learn and grow.

However, these lessons have a way of returning throughout life, especially when we avoid learning them. In a sense, each exit ramp eventually loops around and puts us back on the same road, only each successive time it may be a little steeper. Life has a way of directing us through the lessons whether we want them or not. When we don't learn them the first time, the lessons may feel harder the next time. The cost of taking an exit ramp means we miss a chance to learn the lesson and develop an important internal resource. It means we hold tightly to something that no longer serves us. We all have resources within us—things like honesty, courage, flexibility, love, and resilience. However, we must learn to use them, develop them, and deploy them. The school of life and the path of purpose call them forth. But the choice is always ours. When we take exit ramps, these resources may lie dormant until we choose to stay on the path and learn to release the aspects of ourselves that are not aligned with our true self.

We come into this world like a diamond that gets covered in coal over time. The diamond is the gift, our unique desire, ability, or beauty we innately offer the world. It is experienced and expressed as the One Voice, an inner yes. The coal is the shadow, the accumulated unconscious habits of thought, word, and deed that interfere with who we truly are. These aspects are born of ego and get in the way of what we want in life. As we

> *We come into this world like a diamond that gets covered in coal over time.*

choose to learn the lessons we are here to learn, the coal undergoes a transformation. We allow pressure and time to do their work until the coal is pressed into a diamond all its own. When this happens, our darkest shadow becomes a bright light. Our unconsciousness becomes awareness, deception gives way to truth telling, fear becomes courage, our apathy flips into action, anger yields to forgiveness, our criticism becomes kindness, our envy emerges as appreciation, our pride turns to humility, and our contempt becomes love. The result of our work is the presence of twin diamonds of inestimable worth sitting at the center of our being. The first is our birthright; the second is ours to learn and earn through deliberate practice.

Not everyone's life path is as grave, dramatic, or steep as the one Tom was on. We are each on a path unique to us. But all of us have lessons to learn while we're here. When we choose to stay on the road, move through our challenges, and release the parts that no longer belong, we grow and gain greater capacity and resources. We learn the lessons we are here to learn. This is always a great success. With new resources in hand, we are better equipped to face the next challenge and become what we were made to be. One of the purposes in

> *One of the purposes in life is to realize our potential. This is not only about what we do, but also about who we become.*

life is to realize our potential. This is not only about what we do, but also about who we become.

A definition of success that includes and prioritizes internal aspects of our self does not invalidate external or material abundance. We must only recognize that the external realm is destined to depart from us one day, whereas the inner dimensions of success are everlasting.

DON'T DEPRIVE US

Jerry, a lean man in his late sixties with gray hair and pale-blue eyes, dying of an aggressive form of cancer, reclined in his hospital bed. The doctors had reached the end of medical interventions, and he was mostly bed-bound on a pain-management protocol. I was a chaplain in the liver unit where he stayed. During his stay I visited him several times. He'd practiced medicine for most of his life, so he understood more about his treatment and prognosis than most patients did. He knew exactly what was going on in his body and why. So each time we talked, he focused on other things. Mostly he would tell stories about his life. At one point, he paused, gazed out the window, and said, "I wasn't perfect, but I tried to be a good person. I helped a lot of people get better. I think that's worth something."

Over the course of our visits he repeated a

variation on this theme more frequently. He held it close to him, as a child might hug a teddy bear. As he revisited his contribution in this world, he found a way to come to terms with the end of life. Jerry's survey of his impact on the world is not specific to him. As a chaplain, I had the unique privilege of spending time with people who had recently been made aware that they were dying sooner than they'd expected. In every case, people engaged in some kind of life review; they focused on the questions *Did I make a difference?* and *Did I live a good life?*

Some call this phenomenon "making peace." I have yet to meet a person who is consciously aware of dying and doesn't engage in it. The question *Did I make a difference?* is not present only during moments of facing our mortality. It finds a way to surface throughout life. If a definition of success includes finding joy and learning our lessons, then a third metric of success would be making an impact on the world. However, we must be careful with this last one. While it matters, it is not ours to determine.

The desire to make a difference in life is baked into our being. It reveals an important truth about our purpose in life. We are here not only to find joy and learn our lessons, but also to make an impact. The One Voice will beckon us on a path of

> *We are here not only to find joy and learn our lessons, but also to make an impact.*

self-development and potential, but it will also lead us in ways that make a contribution. We may not always be fully aware of our impact, but when guided by the One Voice from within, a contribution no matter how small is unavoidable and always worth more than we can imagine.

You may recall an estimated 160 billion people have lived on the face of the earth since the dawn of human history. As part of that number you are truly one of a kind. No one else has ever been like you, and no one else will ever be like you. That means everything you do, every choice you make, is a unique expression and contribution in the world.

If you are living according to the One Voice, you will naturally serve others, even if you can't see how, why, or to what extent. In fact, this is the final trick in living your purpose—to become truly divested of outcomes, to learn to release your expectations and trust what comes. This means learning the simple joy of creating and offering as an expression of your highest self and true purpose.

If you are living according to the One Voice, you will naturally serve others, even if you can't see how, why, or to what extent.

Martha Graham was a renowned dancer and choreographer who pioneered modern dance in America. She is said to have been to dance what

Picasso was to visual art, Stravinsky was to music, or Einstein was to math and science. In her biography, *Martha: The Life and Work of Martha Graham* by Agnes de Mille, Graham is quoted as saying:

> There is a vitality, a life force, a quickening that is translated through you into action, and because there is only one of you in all time, this expression is unique. And if you block it, it will never exist through any other medium and be lost. The world will not have it. It is not your business to determine how good it is, nor how valuable it is, nor how it compares with other expressions. It is your business to keep it yours clearly and directly, to keep the channel open. You do not even have to believe in yourself or your work. You have to keep yourself open and aware directly to the urges that motivate you. Keep the channel open.

Few statements better articulate what it means to live our purpose. Graham makes clear that our business is not to be a judge of our own work. Our business is to remain open and committed to offer what we've been given. Our only job is to "keep the channel open." No shortage of barriers exists for this endeavor: white noise, self-limiting beliefs, invented responsibilities, and enmeshed relationships all play a part. The practice of silence and solitude, testing our assumptions about reality, and learning to stand on our own two feet are all antidotes to these barriers. But all of them are fueled by something deeper—a courageous quest to keep the channel open.

Finally, with the channel flowing freely, life compels us to act. Feeling and naming the deepest desire are not enough; the real work of living our purpose happens when we activate our courage, make a decision, and move.

Your deepest desire is a gift life gives you. Following it is your gift to yourself, and the outcome is your gift to the world. By living your deepest desire or purpose, you will experience joy and pleasure beyond measure. But the purpose you've been given isn't just for you. It's for us, too. To live anything less than your deepest purpose, you deprive the world of your greatest gift. Don't deprive us of the gift you're here to offer.

> *Your deepest desire is a gift life gives you. Following it is your gift to yourself, and the outcome is your gift to the world.*

In those moments when you live your purpose courageously, we thank you.

GRATITUDES

I want to express my deepest appreciation for the people who played some part in the creation of this book.

To Joey Paul, my editor at Hachette. This book would never have seen the light of day if you hadn't recovered the project from purgatory, believed in the vision, and coaxed it back to life. Your openness and flexibility as it evolved was critical to the final product.

To Chris Ferebee, my agent. Thank you for all the ways you have hung in there with me through the various twists and turns of my own journey of purpose.

To my children, Harper (age nine) and Hadley (age six), who furnished me with many examples in the book. More than this, at the time of this writing they are at an age when their true self naturally shines through unobstructed. Thank you for providing a clear picture of what it means to know who you are. Life will present you with countless opportunities to abandon yourself. Remember who you were during this time—it will give you important clues in life.

To my mom. Thank you for your close reading of the manuscript, your skilled editorial sense, and the many conversations about the mystery of being human, which helped clarify my thinking. To my dad. Thank you for your support and enthusiasm.

To all the people I have coached. Thank you for allowing me the privilege of entering your world and learning just how remarkable human beings really are. You have taught me there is no limit to our potential.

To the mentors and teachers who have guided me in my understanding of life and sharpened my attention to the One Voice: Prem Rawat, Judith Favor, Sam Alibrando, Jim McNeish, Sonia Choquette, Sonia Tully, Tim Gallwey, and Esther and Abraham Hicks. Thank you for sharing your wisdom.

To Bahar, my beloved partner in life and work. Thank you for your inspiration, challenge, and keen editorial eye. As a fellow writer, it is such a joy to share this creative endeavor. Thank you for all the ways you support me in my purpose. Jooneman. Eschegheman.

NOTES

1. Esther Hicks, *The Astonishing Power of Your Emotions: Let Your Feelings Be Your Guide.* New York: Hayhouse, 2008.
2. Gene Weingarten, "Pearls Before Breakfast." *Washington Post*, April 8, 2007.
3. For a deeper understanding of systems theory and relationships see Roberta M. Gilbert, *Extraordinary Relationships: A New Way of Thinking about Human Interactions.* Minneapolis: Chronimed Pub., 1992; and Edwin H. Friedman, Margaret M. Treadwell, and Edward W. Beal, *A Failure of Nerve: Leadership in the Age of the Quick Fix.* New York: Seabury Books, 2007.
4. Karen Horney, *Our Inner Conflicts: A Constructive Theory of Neurosis.* London: Routledge & K. Paul, 1949. See also Sam Alibrando, *Follow the Yellow Brick Road: How to Change for the Better When Life Gives You Its Worst.* Lincoln, NE: iUniverse Inc., 2007.
5. For a thorough treatment of the dynamics of relational gridlock, emotional fusion, and A-frame relationships in marriage, see David Schnarch, *Intimacy and Desire: Awakening the Passion in Your Relationship.* New York: Beaufort Books, 2011.
6. For a comprehensive introduction to the Enneagram, see Don Riso and Russ Hudson, *The Wisdom of the Enneagram:*

The Complete Guide to Psychological and Spiritual Growth for the Nine Personality Types, 11th edition. New York: Bantam, 1999. An equally helpful but slightly different kind of introduction is Richard Rohr, *The Enneagram: A Christian Perspective.* Chestnut Ridge, NY: The Crossroads Publishing Company, 2001.

7. These questions come from Tim Gallwey, *The Inner Game of Work: Focus, Learning, Pleasure, and Mobility in the Workplace.* New York: Random House. 2001. This is an excellent resource for improving performance in work in a fresh way.
8. The field of neurolinguistic programming is a good resource for understanding our perceptual filters. See Robert Dilts, *Sleight of Mouth: The Magic of Conversational Belief Change.* Capitola, CA: Meta Publications, 1999. See also Joseph O'Connor, *An Introduction to NLP Neuro-Linguistic Programming: Psychological Skills for Understanding and Influencing People.* Thorsons, 1998.
9. Michael Finkel, "The Blind Man Who Taught Himself to See." *Men's Journal*, March 2011.

WORKSHOPS

Shane Hipps offers workshops about purpose and human potential for those interested in taking the practices in this book further. For more information visit www.shanehipps.com/#contact and sign up for his e-mail list to get the latest news and be alerted when workshops are offered. Your e-mail will be kept confidential. Or you can scan the QR code below with a reader on your phone to be directed to the site to sign up.